'This is a funny, valiant and vital book.'

The Listener

'. . . a sparkling autobiography, which deserves to be cherished as fondly as *The Young Visiters* . . . Miss Wyndham charms with innocence, originality, perceptiveness and candour.'

The Sunday Times

'She is an apostle of common sense, a funny woman who abhors solemnity and pretence and writes with iconoclasitc flair.'

The Evening Standard

'. . . delightfully witty, disarmingly candid and idiosyncratically stylish.'

The Sunday Telegraph

Also published in the National Trust Classics

In Search of English Gardens by John Claudius Loudon
Recollections of Rossetti by Hall Caine
William Beckford by James Lees-Milne
The Mitred Earl by Brian Fothergill
In a Gloucestershire Garden by Canon Ellacombe
Felbrigg, the Story of a House by R. W. Ketton–Cremer

The Honourable Ursula Wyndham gives a spirited account of the country house way of life that in fiction has so entranced the readers of Nancy Mitford and Molly Keane. With wit and style she shows us a world where the pleasures of privilege were enjoyed in a peculiarly English way: her mother distrusted all foreigners below the rank of Ambassador, and her grandmother kept the accounts for a house for fallen woman . . .

Made up of her own life and the exploits some of her illustrious ancestors, such as the third Lord Egremont who 'was impatient of the petty details of life, thus forgetting to marry the mother of his children until after they were born', Ursula Wyndham's bitter-sweet world is that of the hunt ball and the uncomfortable house party.

This is her first book. Although there are moments of sadness, it is written, finally, to make the reader laugh out loud.

ASTRIDE THE WALL

A MEMOIR 1913-1945

URSULA WYNDHAM

CENTURY
LONDON SYDNEY AUCKLAND JOHANNESBURG
in association with the National Trust

First published in Great Britain in 1988 by Lennard Publishing, a
division of Lennard Books Ltd.

Published in paperback in 1990 by Century
An imprint of Random Century Ltd
20 Vauxhall Bridge Road, London SW1V 2SA

Century Hutchinson Australia (Pty) Ltd
20 Alfred Street, Milsons Point, Sydney, NSW 2061, Australia

Century Hutchinson New Zealand Ltd
PO Box 40–086, 32–34 View Road, Glenfield, Auckland 10, New
Zealand

Century Hutchinson South Africa (Pty) Ltd
PO Box 337, Bergvlei 2012, South Africa

Printed and bound in Great Britain by The Guernsey Press,
Guernsey

British Library Cataloguing in Publication data

Wyndham, Ursula, 1913–
Astride the wall: a memoir, 1913 – 1945. – (National Trust classics).
1. England. Upper classes. Social life, 1913 – 1945
I. Title II. Series
942.08308621

ISBN 0 7126 3766 4

CONTENTS

	FAMILY TREE	6
	LIST OF ILLUSTRATIONS	8
	PROLOGUE	9
1	THE EDWARDIAN PARENT	13
2	WHAT FORMED EDWARDIAN PARENTS	29
3	FLORENCE COURT – AN ULSTER TIME WARP	45
4	CHANGING VALUES	65
5	BROUGHT UP AND BROUGHT OUT	73
6	THE COUNTRY HOUSE VISIT	101
7	MAKING HAY WHILE THE SUN SHONE	113
8	FATHERS AND DAUGHTERS	129
9	WAR CORRESPONDENCE	141
	EPILOGUE	187
	INDEX	189

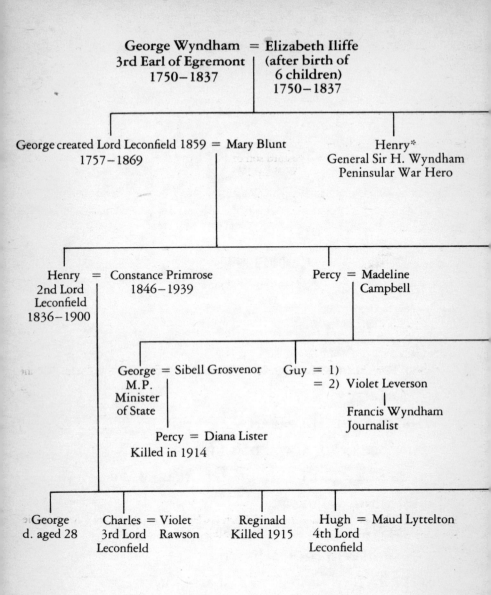

George Wyndham = Elizabeth Iliffe
3rd Earl of Egremont | (after birth of
1750–1837 | 6 children)
1750–1837

George created Lord Leconfield 1859 = Mary Blunt
1757–1869

Henry*
General Sir H. Wyndham
Peninsular War Hero

Henry = Constance Primrose
2nd Lord 1846–1939
Leconfield
1836–1900

Percy = Madeline
Campbell

George = Sibell Grosvenor
M.P.
Minister
of State

Guy = 1)
= 2) Violet Leverson

Francis Wyndham
Journalist

Percy = Diana Lister
Killed in 1914

George
d. aged 28

Charles = Violet
3rd Lord Rawson
Leconfield

Reginald
Killed 1915

Hugh = Maud Lyttelton
4th Lord
Leconfield

* *General Wyndham shut the gate at Hougoumont, the farmhouse that was the
headquarters of the English at the start of the battle of Waterloo. Since his time, it is said,
no Wyndham shuts a door.*

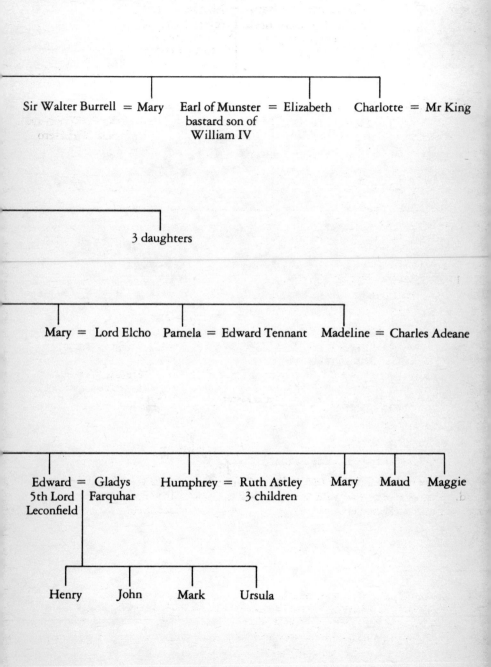

Sir Walter Burrell = Mary   Earl of Munster = Elizabeth   Charlotte = Mr King
                             bastard son of
                             William IV

3 daughters

Mary = Lord Elcho   Pamela = Edward Tennant   Madeline = Charles Adeane

Edward = Gladys   Humphrey = Ruth Astley   Mary   Maud   Maggie
5th Lord   Farquhar   3 children
Leconfield

Henry   John   Mark   Ursula

PROLOGUE

*I*N THE CLOSING years of the 20th century it may be of interest to look back at the period between the Wars, when all classes were feeling the effects of the late hostilities, and the hitherto staid royal family was rocked by transatlantic social crisis; a period when the habits, dictated by what I prefer to call tribal customs rather than class barriers, were more clearly defined and understood; to look, too, at the genetic results of Victorian hypocrisy and Edwardian materialism on a world whose values still continue to change.

Although most stately homes are now opened to inspection under the aegis and publicity of the National Trust, instead of being open free of charge by their owners, as was formerly the case, long-established families still continue to inhabit their ancestral homes. It has to be admitted that the park wall that encloses the stately property has rendered those who continue to live behind it not quite the same as you and I. The park wall, to this day, cuts them off from the generality of the human race. Those who have the curious feeling that they are on the wrong side of the wall arrange with themselves and each other to think that a wine and cheese party held for charity, within the sacred precincts, is tantamount to dining with the Family. This makes an unbridgeable gulf in ease of social intercourse and the sharing of mutual values. The intellectual bourgeoisie is stunned by the lack of knowledge of the artistic or even monetary value of his ancestral possessions divulged by the local lord. This quaint lack of erudition is generously ascribed, by those not to be deprived of their venture into so-called U life, to eccentricity. Without this endearing characteristic the whole of the aristocracy would be up the creek.

I formed, some years ago, one of a party of members of The Georgian Group who had the privilege of being escorted round a fine mansion in Northamptonshire by the owner. We ladies were togged out in our flowered prints and white shoes, with handbags to match; the gentlemen in blazers and neatly pressed trousers. Our host advanced towards us clad in baggy flannel trousers, a tweed jacket that must have been at least thirty years old, but I think his shirt, probably bought by his wife, had come from Turnbull & Asser. He was genial.

"Awfully decent of you all to come," he told us. "I can't think why you have," he added candidly, after a pause for thought. "I'm fond of this house, it's my home, don'cher know, but there is nothing very special about it."

Fearful to contradict, we followed him, awestruck, into the dining room, where every object was a miracle of craftmanship and art.

"Nothing very much here," announced the proud owner. "That cup in the middle of the table was won by my grandfather with a devilish good little horse that he bred." He looked about him, seeking further inspiration from the furnishings that were almost invisible to him from long habitation. "This is rather a jolly picture," he suggested. "Always been fond of it; that's a fine red coat the fellah's wearing, isn't it?"

Somebody ventured to ask who had painted the picture, mid-eighteenth century in style. "Who painted it? Oh, it's no good asking me questions like that. Mind you, my wife would know. It's just rather a jolly picture."

I was rapidly falling in love with a type that I recognised, but seldom met with.

There is a wide-spread human instinct to trace one's ancestral roots back as far as possible. I owe to an aunt (whom I share with Humphrey Lyttelton) with an enthusiastic and informed interest in family legend, my concern with human nature in its successive manifestations down the generations, which leaves us with the certainty that it is a facet of ourselves that does not change: the variations are in the background against which lives pass.

To explore houses, lovingly designed to the highest degree of artistic symmetry, and to speculate on the joy and anguish experienced in the lives of their former inhabitants, is to add a missing dimension to the scene. I have attempted to add that element with regard to some of these houses and to extend it into modern times, where the illusion prevails that the mores of the upper crust no longer exist.

The accent in the hugely successful *Brideshead Revisited* was nostalgia for a way of life and a mode of thought that are as dead as the dodo. Paradoxically, when the background is founded on the glittering apparatus of tremendous wealth, as in *Dallas* and *Dynasty*, it is entirely acceptable.

A kindly man, connected with the production of plays for television, read a play of mine and patiently explained why it was unsuitable for production: the characters were all upper class. When I had recovered my breath, I attempted to point out to him that the woman round whom the plot revolved was married to an ultra-conventional white-collar worker, had no help in the house, and her husband addressed her mother as "Mother-in-law". The latter was entirely concerned with promoting her family to appear to others as in a superior mould.

"Nonetheless," he proclaimed, "she had an upper class background."

Here, I decided, was yet another of those middle-class minded characters, uncertain of their standing, unable to rely on their own individuality in the conduct of their life. I checked on him. He was the son of a landed baronet whose title had been a family handle since 1730.

He had allowed himself to be brainwashed by the system.

THE EDWARDIAN
PARENT

*I*N THE YEAR of my birth, 1913, my father bought an absurdly large, dignified house in Northamptonshire, called Laxton. It stood in the middle of a large, dignified park. I presume my father visualised it as the future ancestral home of a cadet branch of the Wyndhams of Petworth.

I remember Laxton with almost unalloyed pleasure. After the War there was not enough money to keep up the garden, which became a wilderness. It was wonderful child country. For the first ten years of my life I ran wild there, spending most afternoons at the home farm, watching the cows being milked, the pigs fed, the horses unharnessed.

Up at the stables I saw Mrs Cook, the groom's wife, breast-feeding her baby at the door of her cottage in the yard. This was tremendous news to convey to my brother, Henry, and our Cole cousins. Unfortunately they all refused to believe me.

"What? Babies are fed from the chest? Don't be so silly. People are like cows and sheep and horses: they feed their babies between their legs."

It was a crushing disappointment. Oh, for a nursing elephant, whose anatomy and habits we were equally unacquainted with!

Luckily, within the year, they came crawling back. Unbelievably, I had been right. The human female was very curiously constructed.

We were a family of four. My brother, Henry, was two years younger than I. Two more sons, John and Mark, followed in 1920 and 1921. Three sons did not absolve my parents, in their own eyes, from the shame of having given birth to a female child. Every time they read in *The Times* that a daughter had been born to one of their friends, they exchanged cries of mournful lamentation for the luckless parents.

"I suppose I must write; but what can I *say?*", my mother would moan.

My youngest brother, Mark, was also lastingly at fault for having been born after my parents had already decided that they had enough children. My own birth had not taken place until six years after my parents married. My mother was fond of saying that she had gone to a doctor to seek advice on how to have a child and had, later, returned to find out how *not* to. The doctor in question was Aarons, a celebrated gynaecologist, whose success in treating infertile women was so great that cynics suspected him of siring the resultant progeny, who were known as "Aarons' children". There are quite a lot of us.

My father's observation on the same subject was that the invaluable Aarons had revealed how to procreate male or female children as required. In my father's words, it involved remaining as continent as a nun till within three days of the menstrual period for the conception of one sex, and cohabiting within three days of the end of the menstrual period for the other. I cannot accurately remember whether it was boys before menstruation and girls immediately afterwards, or the other way round. To pedants who stated that a woman would not conceive at all at those times, my father pointed out that he had three children to disprove that theory.

My parents met at the Yorkshire home of Lord Galway, Serlby Hall. Their names are recorded in the visitors' book in the year 1906: "Edward Wyndham" and "Gladys Farquhar". Her mother, "Ada Farquhar", was, of course, also present as chaperone. My father admired my mother's stylish grace and social ease. At that period the fact that she was penniless did not frighten him off, as in those halcyon Edwardian days he could not visualise a situation — like a world war, for instance—that would decimate his more than adequate fortune. He fell in love with her. For the rest of his life all his letters to her opened with the words: "My own darling Gladys Mary."

I do not think that my mother ever fell in love. Any situation involving vulnerability was not for her. Twin brothers, called Bonsor, are reputed to have proposed to her at the same ball. My mother said "No" to the first proposal and "Is this supposed to be funny?" to the second. Throughout her life she made that response to most jokes. There is no reason to suppose that young Bonsor was not serious, but my mother would never have married anybody who made a social gaffe.

She was also wooed by an Irish earl. But who wants to fritter their life away on a bog? My father, although a younger son, had money and a stately home behind him. Yet she turned him down twice. Was she looking for something better? My father, at twenty-four, was still under the impression (which soured him so much when he discovered it to be an illusion) that he could get anything he wanted. He said, imperturbably, that he would go on proposing until she said yes. At his third attempt he got his way. She ruled him, but she was punctilious in seeing to his comforts and interests, except when they clashed with her own. Even then she wove some spell to have him suppose her plan was for the best. She was a very efficient woman.

They were married on October 14, 1907.

My mother always found it difficult to enter into childish pleasures. She had a total unrecall of anything she had done when *she* was a little girl, so bedtime stories were practically an impossibility. She read us a chapter from the Bible, rather self-consciously, on Sunday, and taught us to ride.

She quite rightly fancied her appearance on a horse, riding side-saddle, in an elegant habit. My father was a nervous rider over fences, but my mother knew no fear. She had an escort in the hunting field in the person of Sir Raymond Greene, who took his own line across country, closely followed by my mother.

Sir Raymond represented a species I have never again encountered. He was immensely fastidious: about his appearance, his
clothes, his horses, what he ate — in fact, about every area of his
very personal life. He never descended into bonhomie or jollity.
His manner was always one of almost princely dignity. He appeared
to have no close men friends, but a quantity of elegant women
friends, all married, whom he treated with unvarying deference.
No hint of scandal ever sullied these relationships.

My mother was known as Gladdie to everybody but Sir
Raymond, who addressed her as Gl*a*dys, with a long *a*. Anything
that my mother and the other ladies required, Sir Raymond
supplied — even a hunter for me when my old one died and my
father refused to expend any of the money he could not bear to
spend on anybody but himself by replacing the animal. Over from
Sir Raymond's stable came a chestnut hunter that Sir Raymond
explained was too slow to be exactly right for him. It was not a
racehorse, but it was a good, free-actioned galloper, and jumped
like a stag. It was the only horse I have ever known that, having
thrown me from its back by some chance in the middle of a hunt,
stopped dead on the spot until I remounted.

Mark, like myself, was constantly made to feel expendable.
Sent down, with John, for the hour with my mother after tea, he
not infrequently returned to the nursery within ten minutes,
announcing that mummy didn't want him. John enjoyed being
read aloud to, which helped to disguise the lack of communication
between mother and children. Mark, unluckily, did not.

My mother had been encouraged to breast-feed her first child,
but was intensely averse to the ritual and did not attempt it with
any of her other children. To my intense surprise and delight I
discovered that, when goaded, I could momentarily even the score
by saying: "Well, what do you expect from a child that has never
known its mother's milk?"

My mother looked guiltily dismayed.

With John and Mark my father was never involved in the
evening sessions. He made little effort to establish an understanding with any of his children, like his father before him. It was
by no means unusual in the generation preceding his. Sir John

Craddock-Hartopp, my mother's grandfather, so terrified his off-spring that they did not recognise him as parent at all. A young Craddock-Hartopp would raise the alarm. "Sir John is coming!", which was the signal for the whole brood to scurry into hiding.

My father, by the reclusiveness that had become a family characteristic since the days of his great grandfather, the shy, autocratic, eccentric, and deeply private 3rd Earl of Egremont—patron and crony of the like minded J. M. W. Turner, clung to the past, distrusted the present, and feared the future, in particular, death. He died a lonely, querulous, frightened old man; un-approachable, because suspicious of everyone's intentions.

In those early days, however, back from the war, he took quite an interest in his first two children, an interest which was not sustained when they developed opinions of their own. On return-ing from hunting he used to talk to us in the bathroom while he had his bath.

At a later period any freedom of expression was sternly put down by our father. On one occasion, he issued from his personal sanctum of the library into the drawing room in time to hear Henry relating to me how a young fellow from Bristol had come out hunting in experimental guise, with the Beaufort Hunt. Enthusiastically over-riding hounds, he incurred the anger of the Duke, who was huntsman, and bellowed at him: "What the devil do you think you are doing, sir?" The Bristolian, unconscious of his crime, replied: "Just taking air and exercise", to which he received the ducal instruction to "go home and bugger himself with the bellows". My father castigated Henry for telling such a story in a drawing room to a woman. Henry's excuse that I was his sister met with the rebuke that our relationship had nothing to do with the matter.

One evening, in the dining room, my astonished ears heard my father relate to himself (my mother never listened to coarse anec-dotes and I was supposed not to understand them) the history of a man travelling by train in a compartment full of pretty girls. He unbuttoned his trousers, drew out "what they concealed" (I think my father expressed himself thus), put his pince-nez upon it and said, "look around, little fellow, and tell me which you fancy".

In spite of his reproof to Henry, it now appeared that it was the room such stories were told in, not the sex of the recipient, that was all-important. My father, a great drinker of port, may have forgotten momentarily that there were no fellow port drinkers present and that the ladies, although silent, had not withdrawn.

Under similar conditions he was fond of holding forth on the subject of poetry and poetic licence. On this topic, too, my mother was a non-listener. She was only interested in subjects that would promote conversation at Bridge and dinner parties. My opinions were never canvassed and not encouraged. So my father told himself, at not infrequent intervals, that Samuel Taylor Coleridge's reference to 'the horned moon, with one bright star within its nether tip' was an instance of the beauty of words taking precedence over the misrepresentation of facts of nature.

Another oft repeated favourite was Christina Rossetti's

In the bleak mid winter
Frosty wind made moan.
Earth stood hard as iron,
Water like a stone.

Stone-like water was, he averred, a particularly potent simile. And what added to the beauty of the image was that, at the reputed season of Christ's birth, a frosty wind would not be making moan in Palestine.

Since I could see no analogy, poetic or otherwise, between a lump of ice and a stone, and thought it destructive to analyse so remorselessly the poet's intention, I would have liked to question my father on why the exercise gave such profound pleasure to him.

As my father disliked dining out, it was understood among their circle that my mother was prepared to leave him at home. All too often, therefore, I had to dine alone with him, which filled me with such dread that it blackened the whole day. What made the ordeal worse was that he talked down to me with elaborate, painstaking and condescending kindness, so that no controversial point ever arose.

My father had commanded the 1st Life Guards, where he

earned the nickname 'Methuselah'. His younger brother not only commanded the same regiment, but went through the Staff College, as well. This one-upmanship irritated my parent. After retirement from the army, he mooched about at home for three years, endeavouring to find fulfilment in a study of ornithology. A business friend came to the rescue and got him a working director-ship in a road construction company. This, to my surprise, entirely satisfied him, and dinners were made even more boring by the addition of lectures on the components of bitumen to his usual repertoire of his increasing impecuniousness, dissecting poetry, thundering against adultery and heaving with laughter at his own jokes.

"There is only one thing worse than having no sense of humour", he was wont to proclaim, "and that is thinking things funny that aren't." The latter comprised all witticisms not uttered by himself.

Much later I learnt that a contemporary of mine, Elizabeth Eliot, of Port Eliot in Cornwall, quite calmly and determinedly had her dinner sent up to her bedroom whenever she felt that the company in the dining room would bore her. Even had I had the courage, I could not have got away with that, as eating alone was a phobia of my father's. None the less, a little cunning fore-thought — a sudden headache or sickness and a confidential word to the maid I shared with my mother, who would have brought a tray to my bedroom — might have spared me at least some of these ordeals.

Rickard, this maid, was a large, taciturn woman, a skilled dressmaker, and a person I implicitly trusted. I had a nappy pony, very apt to whip round without warning, whom I thought I could control. However, one day, after a very hard hunt in the morning, the run ended with the pony I was riding exhausted, within a mile of home. I had the wicked chestnut one saddled and rode out of the stable yard to rejoin the hunt. I was cantering down the side of the high road to catch up with them . . . .

My next memory is of walking in the other direction up the road, without the slightest idea of how I had got there. To my immense relief, I discovered, upon reflection, that I knew what my name was and where I lived, but among other losses of recollection I could not remember what day of the week it was. The importance of knowing what day of the week it was assumed mammoth proportions in my mind. I flagged down a coal lorry with the riding whip that was still in my hand — so I presumed that the whip, combined with the fact that I was booted and spurred, meant that I had been out hunting when the event that I could not remember had occurred. I asked the lorry driver to take me home, a distance of about two miles. What I wanted much more to ask him was what day of the week it was, but I feared he would think I was mad.

We had a slight altercation as he drove through the lodge gates. He wanted to deliver me to the back door. It was the entrance that for all daily purposes I used; but my concussed head felt that when one approached the house by motor transport, even if it was a coal lorry, the front door was where one drove to. The driver gave way rather reluctantly, and put me down at the front door. I rang the bell before entering the house, in order to ask the parlourmaid to send Rickard to me, in my bedroom. When she came I hastened to ask the day of the week. Nothing else mattered. She replied "Wednesday", as if it was the most natural question in the world to be asked in the middle of the afternoon.

The lady's maid was a feared figure in the household. Fashionable women, who felt the need to have their maid about them to help with their hair-styling, made confidantes of these invaluable assistants and, since confidences are apt to run in two directions, it was feared the lady's maid would report on any little peccadilloes being enacted on the far side of the green baize door.

My mother was popular with her employees, because she had no favourites and treated every member of her staff exactly the same. The only person who did not like the treatment was myself, who shared it. Asked to fetch a handkerchief from her bedroom, I would gladly do so. It would be taken from my hand in total silence.

Just once, I pointed out that a word of thanks would be appreciated. My mother remained silent and expressionless for a few embarrassing moments. She then articulated "Thank you" in the coldest of monotones. It is a genetic fault. One of my nieces has it. I still do not like it.

It must be pointed out that those brought up behind park walls were not taught good manners or a sense of consideration for others, apart from that, in getting very little consideration them-selves, they early understood what it is like to follow a code of rules already laid down and from which any variation receives strong discouragement.

A set of very spurious rules emanated from the nursery and schoolroom. Nannies insisted that their charges always said "please" and "thank you" automatically — not as though these words had any meaning. Governesses promoted an intricate code of table manners, never met with subsequently in the dining room. This code entailed passing to each other eatables that were within easy reach of everybody without this officious display. For some possibly ancient voodooesque reason, nobody must be the first to put anything into their mouths. By the same token it was necessary to ask those who did not want salt and pepper whether, in fact, they did, before helping oneself. Basically the code seemed to indicate that it was dangerous, as well as ill-mannered, ever to act indepen-dently, even if the act only took a second to perform.

Nannies' teaching was retained, though with the later acquired ingredient of gratitude, a grace not inculcated at any stage of upbringing. I think it safe to say that every precept instilled by a governess, of which snobbery ranked high on the list, was rightly and properly and instinctively dropped as soon as the short influence of these repressed and unhappy women was removed.

The total lack of imagination and self-promotion exhibited by the five governesses with whom I came in contact (three concerned, with a marked lack of success, in my own education, one in that of my brothers, and my cousins the Coles' dismal mademoiselle) still fills me with astonishment. True, they were totally isolated. Parents left them in sole command of the schoolroom and treated them with the distant civility they extended to the domestic staff. The governess was intent on proving her gentility, but nobody was interested. The servants were aware of the pretensions of she who presided in the schoolroom, and were in a strong position to put the governess in her place: she was, after all, just another paid employee. If the schoolroom bell rang, there was no necessity for answering it. They counted on the governess not complaining to her employer, since in so doing she would be betraying her lack of control over a situation — which would sow the seed of doubt as to whether, therefore, she was fit to exercise control over her charges. Never did these women attempt to discuss their pupils' educational progress, or lack of it, with the parents, in order to build a bridge of mutual interest. Still less, of course, would they establish a good relationship with the servants.

The standard of food served up at nursery meals was unprecedented in its inedibility. I think my personal interest in cooking is an offshoot of bitter memories of what we were forced to eat, with revulsion, in those far-off days: greasy mutton, overcooked vegetables wallowing in much of the water they had been boiled in; burnt rice puddings, and, worst of all, tapioca puddings. Sometimes a bowl of tinned fruit appeared as extra largesse: it took less time to open a tin than to peel and core fresh fruit. This prison fare was the unsupervised production of the kitchen maid, whose more important task was to assist the cook in preparing many courses for the dining room twice a day. As like as not the girl was also coping with the unwished-for shock of pregnancy.

Overshadowing all these other aspects of my early life was a fear of the workhouse. Not fear in the sense of terror, since I had learnt that there was nobody to share terror with. There was the terror of the bogeyman, for instance, who lived in the housemaids' cupboard at the foot of the nursery stairs at Laxton; terror on being banished from the night nursery to a room of my own on a mezzanine floor, half-way up the nursery stairs and directly above the bogeyman's cupboard: a room, moreover, that had a wallpaper of what I was sure were tigers glaring out of the jungle foliage. One had, by hook or by crook, to grapple with terror alone.

No, the persistent fear derived from my father's habit of fulminating, at regular intervals, that he was ruined. Naturally, ruin led to the workhouse. Where else?

In 1929 these parental cries intensified and action — action, I feared, of a drastic nature — had to be taken.

24

In the event it was an anti-climax. Mr Green, the smarmy butler, was dismissed and his duties, including acting as valet to my father, were undertaken by a starched, efficient parlourmaid, inhuman as an automaton, who was paid a lower wage. My mother made her sacrifice as well. She cancelled her subscription to the two society weeklies, the *Tatler* and the *Sketch*. I was left without a horse to hunt, but Sir Raymond Greene, like a good angel, took care of that deficiency. Otherwise life continued exactly as before — including my father's cries of impending ruin.

In temperament Henry was entirely different from both his sister and his two brothers. He was, in fact, a law unto himself and our parents stood in considerable awe of him, as of a changeling.

He had always wanted to be a soldier. My father, who had a mania that nobody but himself should benefit from the little money that he considered remained to him of his pre-war fortune, vetoed this ambition with the injunction that it was Henry's duty to apprentice himself to some profession that would quickly make him financially independent. The subalterns in crack regiments had a high standard of living and depended on generous financial allowances from their fathers. Foiled of the only ambition he had, Henry joined the Leicestershire Yeomanry as a part-time soldier. The annual camp was very popular with the local yeomen. Henry borrowed two of his father's hunters and the head-groom's son, Sid. They rode away together. Much joy has gone out of soldiering since the passing of the Cavalry as such.

Henry remained silent on the subject of being debarred from following the profession of his choice, but our father was made subtly aware of a certain slipperiness in Henry's approach to alternative parental plans for a lucrative career. It ended in Henry ostensibly attaching himself to the personnel in control of some-body's broad acres in Yorkshire to learn estate management. This position gave easy access to all the racecourses and packs of hounds in England and Ireland.

Many were the stories narrated on his home forays. I was particularly interested in a family of sisters called Foot, known collectively as the Feet. One Foot, it appeared, was quite good-looking. The other Feet seemed to be unworthy of consideration.

Unknown to him, this lofty generalisation confirmed, in his sister's mind, that unless you looked like Lady Diana Cooper, of the previous generation, or Miss Rose Bingham[1] of ours, it was useless to expect to be adored by a glamorous man, and distasteful to be adored by anything less.

Henry and I played, at weekends, with our friends, a game that now strikes me as singularly fatuous, but which continued to be in favour during the War in a slightly emended form. We turned over the pages of the bound copies of *Country Life* in our parents' library and awarded ourselves marks for either knowing or being related to the social celebrities whose photograph appeared on the opening page.

On 10 November 1942, Mark wrote to me from Egypt where he was serving with the M.E.F.:

> I must have told you of Captain Mesa's game by now, but just in case I haven't it is called 'At Random'. You open the *Peerage* anywhere – at random – and read out the names of those inside and assess accordingly: if it is a Duke, how well you know him, if you stay with him, etc. Peter Willes[2] and Geoffery Nares[2] used to play the whole time. We subtracted marks from Peter for knowing Lord Donegal.[3] It is a good game I think played without the *Peerage*, and played the whole time; just scoring marks for people who crop up in conversation. We try and score marks by talking to Generals in the Desert and pretending we know them well. Peter lost a lot of marks one week when an old concert party actress in Alexandria hailed him as an old friend. Peter tried to make out she was scoring marks with her friend by talking to him. A game I play with Michael de Pino, another of my low friends, is marking everyone, including oneself. For instance, Freeman gets 8 out of 10 for being very nice and in the Rifle Brigade. A gunner major gets only 4, because his hair is cut like a convict and he talks a lot of drivel. Michael and I find that

---

[1] Married: 1933–38 the Earl of Warwick; 1938–40 William Fiske; 1945–50 John Lawson; 1951 Theodore Basset.
[2] Both actors. G. Nares was killed. P. Willes became a television producer.
[3] A Gossip-columnist.

we both usually get 100 out of a possible 2 for being so far ahead of anyone else. Some of the ladies one sees dancing in Cairo get minus marks and are metaphorically turned outisde. One night, several heard us giving this order of 'outside' and were a trifle puzzled.

I rifled through the pages of the *Peerage* to find myself a husband and settled on Sir Aymer Maxwell of Monreith; he was a suitable age and of the same family as the notorious Jane, Duchess of Gordon, who raised a regiment. A grander title would have involved one in a tedious lifetime of opening bazaars.

My mother, while agreeing with my father that nobody would look twice at their daughter, was on tenterhooks as to what sort of women might snare her sons. Henry took pleasure in not allowing her anxiety any respite. To a certain extent I was in his confidence, as is shown in a letter of his to me, written after the outbreak of War from a training camp, while still serving with the Leicester-shire Yeomanry.

> I am not engaged to Miss Brodrick, nor so far as I know have I ever been. She was at one time engaged to Eric Penn but he refuses to marry while a War is on, with which I thoroughly agree, if you knew the terrible lives these wives lead dragging round after their husbands who never have time to go near them, you would also. I have given Gwinny a ring but it was an eternity not an engagement ring. I was unaware she is knitting me a pullover but shall be very grateful to receive it. I should like my mother to be told as it would be very funny especially as she does not like Gwinny. Don't go round telling anybody else as it isn't true. I would have you know that Miss Brodrick is a millionairess and mark my words you will pray for a brother married to a millionairess after the War, still I have not yet descended so low as marrying for cash, the more especially as it has always been my conviction that I shall be killed in this war.

Henry's intimation of his own death was justified. He was killed at the Battle of El Alamein. In him I lost an irreplaceable ally.

WHAT FORMED
EDWARDIAN PARENTS

ART PATRON, eccentric, agriculturist, philanthropist, George O'Brien Wyndham, third Earl of Egremont, was a true child of the 18th century. He kept open house for anybody who cared to visit him, the only stipulation being that the guests must not expect any irksome duties of hospitality from their host. They were at liberty to make what demands they chose of his large, unorthodox and undisciplined staff.

Although Lord Egremont was eighty-six years old when death claimed him in 1837, it has been reported that his end was hastened by the shock of discovering that his retainers and dependents had been consistently robbing him. Anyone so impatient of the petty but essential details of life—such as, for instance, forgetting to marry the mother of his children until after they were born, when he has a noble heritage to hand on—cannot surely have been surprised at the obvious consequences of such a mode of life.

He was succeeded at Petworth by his eldest bastard son, George, who had started life under his mother's name of Iliffe. Gradually the thin end of the wedge of respectability was inserted and Lord Egremont's bastards progressed from Iliffe-Wyndham till they finally felt sufficiently secure to drop the Iliffe entirely.

George was created Lord Leconfield in 1859, but the slur of

bastardy made him a shy, unapproachable man all his life. With him the 19th century prejudices and mode of life took over at once. He married Mary Blunt, the strictly Evangelical daughter of a clergyman, who was the doubtless disapproving aunt of the reprobate Wilfrid Scawen Blunt (invariably written of as an aristocrat, which he had no pretensions to be).

Of Lord Leconfield's two sons, Henry and Percy, the younger son, Percy, was his father's acknowledged favourite. It became an established thing that, even after he married Madeline Campbell, Percy, with family, spent about six months of the year at Petworth, his every whim indulged. Henry bore it patiently during his father's lifetime, but after the old man's death, Percy took it for granted that the long-established custom should continue. What must have been an added irritation for Henry was that his wife, Constance, and Percy's wife Madeline, were inseparable friends. This friendship was undoubtedly made closer and more interdependent on account of a view held by both brothers: "I must be allowed to do as I like".

Intermittent quarrels were part of the brotherly Petworth scene, and were tactfully deflated by the wives. Until, out of a cloudless sky, Henry, in a rage, ordered Percy out of the house, with all his family — at once.

Madeline wrote a distraught letter to Constance asking her if she could possibly find out what had caused this sudden banishment, as Percy claimed to be quite unconscious of having given occasion for displeasure in any form. Constance wrote despairingly back that she had questioned Henry closely on the subject of what had caused his rage. He had replied that he could not remember, but that Percy and Madeline were on no account to return and, furthermore, that the two wives were to cease all correspondence. Constance's acute distress at this order is manifest. In her final letter she writes of all Madeline means to her in friendship, loyalty, support, sympathy, and mutual understanding. She cannot visualise life bereft of this ever-available crony.

The rift lasted a year, after which reconciliation was gradually brought about by the wives. The story highlights a situation not uncommon among Victorian women who, however much they

32

were the centre of the social scene, remained, *au fond*, victims of their husbands' malice. In cases such as that of Constance and Madeline, who were women of great intelligence, we may guess that their latent influence may well have been greater than mere facts reveal.

Henry Leconfield and Percy Wyndham had a mentally retarded sister, but she was never permitted to be an inconvenience. The family despatched her to spend each day with the rector and his wife, who were asked, in rather insufficient recompense, to lunch on Sundays.

It was understandable if Henry was jealous of Percy, who was better looking, more intelligent and very popular and successful, with his beautiful wife, in the social and political scene of the period. The couple's three beautiful daughters were painted by Sargent, draped with elegant languor all over a sofa. The picture, known as *The Three Graces*, now hangs in the largest picture gallery in New York.[1]

I want to single out Mary, the one sitting on the back of the sofa, for further comment. She suffered all her adult life from unrequited love for Arthur Balfour. Ardent by nature, it soon became an obsession with her. And she could not have selected a worse subject for her adoration.

A. J. Balfour was the hero of the expression 'Bob's your uncle'. His mother's brother, the 2rd Marquess of Salisbury, had headed the Government three times as Prime Minister. Not unnaturally, there were people who felt that if *they* had an uncle Bob, highly placed in affairs of State, *their* path to fame would have been as pleasantly paved and easy to set foot on.

I have to confess to an antipathy to Balfour. To my mind he felt born to make some woman unhappy and was waiting, like a snake, to strike at his victim. He enjoyed making himself very agreeable to the female sex and they found him undeniably charming while, barring the over-susceptible Mary, keeping out of reach of the poisoned dart. He had some sexual hang-up which must be taken

---

[1] 'The Wyndham Sisters' by John Singer Sargent (1900). Now in the Metropolitan Museum of Art, New York.

into account in assessing his intimate relationships and his whole temperament as it developed.

Such men often find their time at University an embarrassing confrontation with their deep-seated inadequacies. Balfour looked back on this period as one of 'Almost unmixed satisfaction' and, in another context, 'on the whole the pleasantest I have ever passed'. This complacency has to bespeak a marked lack of imagination, or he would have realised that he was, in fact, announcing that the rest of his life had been a long, slow anti-climax.

He made many friends among both the undergraduates and the dons. John Strutt and Henry Sidgwick, whom he invited to his family home, Whittingham, East Lothian, married his sisters, Evelyn and Eleanor. Sidgwick, who had the attractive characteristics of quickness of wit and a gentle sense of humour, was impotent. Did anyone think to warn Miss Balfour? I doubt it. I can cite two other cases where this rather necessary information was not imparted to the bride prior to the marriage.

She was suited to her role in that she once confessed regretfully that she doubted if she had ever been excited in her life. If she felt the lack of completeness in her marriage, her brother would appear to have been ignorant of it. Like the Sydney Webbs, the Sidgwicks worked together untiringly for the spread of education.

Beatrice Webb, who had to conquer her love for Joseph Chamberlain because she did not fancy playing second fiddle to a great man, has recorded that being the beloved of a dozen of the ablest men would greatly expand a woman's knowledge of human nature and human affairs: 'Since such a relationship would include physical intimacy, with all the consequent pertubations, it is doubtful whether you would have any brain left to think with'. Thoughtlessly discarding the knowledge of human nature without which mankind wanders alone through the labyrinth of life, Balfour followed Mrs Webb's precept to the letter.

Tradition asserts that Balfour confessed to having once experimented in the art of sexual intercourse and found it not an art, but a nasty, messy business. All right: the act cannot accurately be described as good, clean fun. But it would be naive to assume his simple statement of fact did not mask a physical problem. As

W. C. Fields said: "Some things may be better than sex and there may be things that are worse, but there is nothing exactly like it." Balfour made the decision to throw every aspect of the unique human experience out of the window of his mind. To achieve this he built up, little by little, fortifications that, at moments, brought his most determined adorer to hysterics and his own spirit to hypocrisy.

The cornerstone of this defence mechanism was May Lyttelton, an attractive, perceptive, intelligent girl, one of the large family of Lord Lyttelton of Hagley, Worcestershire. She judged Balfour as 'certainly very clever and very much unlike other people, which may be affectation and conceit'. Later she decided: 'he dangles about and does nothing to an extent which becomes wrong... though I like him very much, only I feel ten years older than him.'

May had already felt the reciprocated attraction of two men who had died. The death of the second, Rutherford Graham, upset her deeply. When she was looking outward once more, her friendship with Balfour became closer, but within a year, in 1875, she herself had succumbed to typhoid, a scourge of the period. Balfour's grief was pointedly blatant for all to see, and, with no one to contradict him, he was safe in saying that, had she lived, he would have married her; which turned into the unspoken comment that he could never, from then on, find room in his heart for anyone else.

His sister and Beatrice Webb led useful and industrious lives working side by side as a team, with kind husbands, like well-yoked oxen. Did Balfour ever ask himself whether the life enhancing May would have settled for such half-measures? By dying, she made it possible to evade this vital question.

All his life women fell for that melancholy, dangling decadence. Balfour gave them every formal encouragement. He enjoyed feminine society. He knew how to pay the compliments that pleased them. Most of his female friends were satisfied married women. The exception was my father's cousin Mary, daughter of Percy and Madeline Wyndham. She fell in love with Balfour on her début at the age of eighteen. She ached to marry him, and told him so; told him, too, of how many other men 'wanted me to wife', as she put it, in the curiously stilted way she expressed herself on paper — which must have been at variance with the natural ardour of her temperament, inherited from her mother, that held nothing back. May Lyttelton, by contrast, wrote with fluency and perception and in natural style. Balfour could, and probably did, make comparisons between their approaches: May's more in tune with circumstances, more intuitive; Mary, totally lacking in tactics and thus feeling at a perpetual disadvantage.

Failing to give herself to Balfour, she allowed herself to be married to Lord Elcho, later Earl of Wemyss, a clever, idle philanderer and gambler. Husband and wife agreeing to go their own ways did not protect Lady Elcho from a married life of perpetual financial and sexual crisis.

It is accepted that most people who wholly sublimate their sexual impulses, while living in a world where other people are having a go at satisfying theirs, are particularly prone to depression and neurosis. They also have problems facing up to disagreeable facts. Balfour's cousin, Jim Salisbury, expressed his cousin's quandary thus: 'As a leader he has never ridden across country, and the besetting sin of always looking for a gate has, I am afraid, done a good deal to debase English public life.' Somebody else wrote of him: 'He thinks it is best to sit hard on one's sympathies and will not look at a paper for fear of seeing a tragedy.' Just as well, because until he learnt, by degrees, to exercise an iron control, his neurosis found sudden furious outbursts.

The first of these was when, in 1886, Laura, the much loved sister of Margot Asquith, and the wife of May's brother and Balfour's friend, Alfred Lyttelton, died in childbirth. All her many friends were devastated; but Balfour went further, by furiously accusing Mary Elcho of not, to his notion, sufficiently participating in the agony that all must feel. This might justly have been the moment for her to join battle in a counter-attack on the objective sacrifice of more properly leaving this province to the heart-broken husband and Laura's close and devoted family. Especially as Balfour may half-consciously have suspected that Mary was secretly relieved that one rival for her adored Arthur's affection was out of the way for ever. Instead, she grovelled to him.

'I feel and know I am dumb and awkward—not a friend though with all the will, but a miserable makeshift of a friend, but if you could really know my thoughts, 'hard' would be the very last word you would apply ... you must forgive me.'

Paradoxically, on another occasion when a dignified acceptance would have been in order, the sophisticated Lady Elcho became hysterical. The beautiful Lady Curzon, devoted to her husband and intent only on furthering his ambitions, was an attractive and undemanding friend in Balfour's orbit, and the recipient of his most charming, beguiling and flattering conversational exchanges while her husband was absent in India. After a weekend at Stanway, the Elchos' home in Gloucestershire, at which both Balfour and Lady Curzon were guests, it would appear that the hostess had made an assignation with Balfour that they should lunch together, tête-à-tête, on the Monday. In the hall, when goodbyes were being exchanged Balfour proposed to Lady Curzon that she should join them. In all innocence she accepted.

Balfour and Lady Curzon arrived at the rendezvous at the appointed hour; Lady Elcho did not. As if forseeing this contingency, Balfour suggested that they did not wait, and proceeded to escort Lady Curzon to their table. From then on he behaved as if Lady Elcho did not exist, ignoring or placating Lady Curzon's increasing anxiety concerning their friend's absence. At the end of the meal Lady Curzon valiantly, in the teeth of Balfour's opposition, insisted that they should both call at Lady Elcho's home and enquire as to her well-being and whereabouts. They were admitted and shown into a room on the ground floor, while the footman went to make enquiries. A moment later Lady Elcho came tearing down the stairs, *en déshabille*, her hair streaming down her back, her body wrapped in a grubby satin dressing gown, her face distraught and without make-up of any kind. She appeared not to notice Lady Curzon, and launched into a passionate disquisition on the subject of Balfour's heartlessness: how seldom did they get an opportunity to be alone together; he had promised that it should be just him and her at luncheon; how could he expect her to take such a betrayal lightly; and on and on and on.

Balfour said absolutely nothing: made no attempt to stem the flow nor offer excuses, far less, comfort. When Lady Elcho had shrieked herself to a stop, he motioned Lady Curzon to leave, which she did, appalled by what she had witnessed.

In 1907, after Lady Curzon was dead, Sydney and Beatrice Webb visited Stanway, where Balfour was a fellow-guest. The experience evoked in Mrs Webb a fantasy of chastity slightly beyond imagination. She wrote, enthralled, of 'the beautiful-natured Mary Elcho — neglected wife, devoted and tenderly-loved mother, and adored friend — a beautiful soul in a delicately refined form.' No hint of grubby dressing gowns and unbearable tension.

Balfour is more justly delineated as a knight in impenetrable armour: 'In his courtly devotion to Lady Elcho, in the intimate and sincere talk about men and thought that seems to be natural to him in her presence, Prince Arthur is at his best. It is clearly an old and persistent sentiment — good sound friendship, with just that touch of romantic regret that it could not have been more, that deepens sex feeling and makes such a relation akin to religious renunciation. One can believe that the relation between these two has always been at the same high level of affectionate friendship, without taint of intrigue.'

Perhaps by then the ardent fire of Mary Elcho's spirit may have been quenched to no more than warm embers glowing in the ashes that Balfour told his sister had taken the place of his heart. It was understood between him and this woman he knew adored him, that each should be the other's cherished confidant, during their whole lifetime. The state between love and friendship, more delightful than either, but more difficult to remain in, and the neurosis said to arise from lack of sexual commitment allied to love, is hauntingly verified in Lady Elcho's experience.

As a very attractive woman, what kept her captive in such an empty cell? We cannot tell. All is hypothesis, speculation, psychological presumption. There is a fleeting suggestion in their letters of flagellation: his guilt, her satisfaction. I have questioned whether a woman of Lady Elcho's breeding and upbringing would descend, even in distress of the acutest kind, to depravity? And what if, I have been answered, loving him as she did, that was the only way that she could make him happy? Argument falters in the face of human need.

She was a fatally fertile woman, well knowing that any sexual encounter would almost certainly result in pregnancy. That practised seducer, Wilfred Scawen Blunt, was determined to prove his own power over Balfour's chaste love. He succeeded, in a spot of his own choosing: the Egyptian desert. Lady Elcho conceived, her husband accepted paternity, but his wife was prostrate with despair at having betrayed Balfour, although she had confided to Blunt that her life's love would not be jealous: he was not like other men. That, at least, must have taken the edge off Blunt's satisfaction.

What I find hardest of all to forgive in Balfour is that he sent to his sister-in-law a letter to be opened in the event of his death, in which, after remarking that she and all whom he loved would be able to talk him over, he continues:

> There is one, however, who will not be in such a position. I want you to give her *as from yourself* {my italics} this little brooch which you will find herewith: and tell her that, at the end, if I was able to think at all, I thought of her. If I was the means of introducing any unhappiness into her life I hope God will forgive me. I know she will.

The 'if' is, to me, the essence of inhumanity.

During my own adolescence and young womanhood certain of my mother's friends made more impact upon my imagination and played a more significant part in the eventual development of my character, and sense of what was due to others in relation to myself, than my parents ever attempted. War severs more relationships than it creates. By the 1920s my mother was no longer on close terms with my two godmothers: Irene Enniskillen and Peggy Crewe. In the same way I and Irene's daughter, Frances, have grown apart, through developing mentally along completely different lines. The severence between my parents and Lord and Lady Crewe must have been of Peggy's making. In the 1920s her husband became British Ambassador to France. An invitation to the Embassy in Paris would have been synonymous with Paradise in my mother's eyes, but it never came.

My mother had four very close female friends: Irene Roberts, Dorothy Graham, Mildred Gosford and Gladys Huntington. Mrs Graham was the wife of Harry Graham, whose book: *Ruthless Rhymes for Heartless Homes* lay on every drawing room table. One such example ran as follows:

> Billy, in one of his nice new sashes,
> Fell in the fire and was burnt to ashes.
> Now, although the room grows chilly,
> We haven't the heart to poke poor Billy.

Such quips are easily committed to memory. They could be, and were, quoted *ad nauseam*. Mildred Gosford, née Carter, and the divorced wife of the 5th Earl of Gosford, was, like Mrs Huntington, wife to Constant Huntington, the head of the English office of the publishing house of Putnam, an American. The first three ladies, immaculately *soignée* and at ease in any situation, took not the slightest notice of me. I enjoyed the company of two of Lady Gosford's four children: Patrick and Mary Acheson. Unfortunately Patrick chose to make his home in his mother's country and Mary married a Mexican.

Mrs Huntington I found totally fascinating. She had a full measure of the Edwardian heartlessness, but leavened by an acute interest in everybody and everything. Her only child, Alfreda, was of an age with John and Mark. She accompanied her parents on visits to Edmondthorpe. Mrs Huntington invaded the nursery, which was more than my mother ever did. With practised charm she put the nanny and nursery maid at their ease. She was wont to strike up conversations in railway carriages and with taxi drivers, becoming, by this means, the recipient of remarkable confidences, which she relayed with zest. I greatly envied and admired this gift. Years later, having conquered my shyness, I emulated it: mostly as an antidote to the fears, hazards and delays involved in air travel. Mrs Huntington was blatantly unashamed of thinking ill of others. "I have my knife into him/her", she was wont to proclaim, adding venomously: "and *turned*!" On my first visit to Florence, she informed me: "You may come across my nephew there. I am not on

40

terms with him. I would not wish to hear that he was happy."

My mother also had three spinster cronies in Dorothy Yorke, Wini Douglas-Pennant and Horatia Seymour. My father rarely had any use for women who had not succeeded in getting married. In spite of Wini Pennant being very pretty, his cold disdain frightened her so much that she prattled aimlessly from sheer terror. Dorothy Yorke was Aunt Maud Yorke's sister-in-law. A jolly extrovert of a woman, she was nonetheless quite unintimidated by my father. Except that she played Bridge and hunted and was a relation by marriage, she did not appear to have much in common with my mother, who set great store by the social graces, which Dorothy could not be bothered to practise. That she was a lady in waiting to the Princess Royal can hardly have been a point in her favour, since the Princess, attended by Dorothy, led a most unglamorous life.

Horatia Seymour, beautiful, indolent, with a dropping-down-deadness of manner, was also intelligent, erudite and the friend of many clever people. She was a law unto herself. Like Ann Cole, she faced whatever odds there were with unconquerable spirit. I came to see her as the best of the bunch and to learn much from her.

Wini and Dorothy were mutual chums. Soon after the end of the War in 1945, Dorothy complained persistently of feeling ill. This was anti-social. If you felt ill, you took to your bed until you felt better. You did not bore people by talking about it. When Dorothy continued to voice her anxiety concerning her health, in spite of medical reassurance, all her friends, including Wini, dropped her. Finally Dorothy went, alone and unattended, into hospital, for an exploratory operation. In the hospital, on the eve of the operation, she took an overdose and killed herself. The post mortem revealed that she was riddled with cancer. I was deeply shocked, but I had the emotion entirely to myself. My mother and her friends, including Dorothy's special chum, Wini, shrugged the whole tragedy off.

I would have liked to visit Dorothy during those last dire months of her life, but I lacked the courage. She had, from time to time, invited me to tea at her flat in Manchester Square, but I did not feel free to knock on her door, uninvited. With Wini my relationship was closer and easier. Armed with books by Augustus Hare and John Summerson, we explored together, by car, little known corners of London. The painted staircase at 8 Clifford Street, the one house remaining of the original design for Hanover Square, in the south west corner, the Savoy Chapel, Lincoln's Inn and its Fields and many byways in the City. We went further afield, to Ham House, Kew Green, Strawberry Hill and, through Wini's effrontery, forced an entry into Claremont, which still is a girls' school. Wini rang the bell and, to my acute embarrassment, said to the school-mistress type who answered it: "I am the Honourable Winifred Douglas-Pennant. I and my friend have a great wish to see this famous and beautiful house..." The woman, unaccustomed to such an approach, understandably went to seek guidance from a superior. Wini then had the grace to say to me: "I am sorry about that, but it does work." It did.

Wini's end was even more horrific, from being more drawn-out, than Dorothy's. With increasing age, Wini, while still enchanting in appearance, became more and more self-centred. She had another friend, like herself an unmarried Honourable, who begged for Wini's company over Christmas, but for which she would have to spend it entirely alone. Wini's reply was that she could not be bothered to make the journey. She had a faithful old maid-servant, both of them by then wracked by arthritis. It was Wini who sat in a darkened room, pressing the bell whenever she wanted anything. The other old cripple uncomplainingly hobbled around, ministering to Wini's every whim. I was so shocked by this manifestation of where excessive self-concern was leading somebody who had been very good company, that I made a point, when I was in London, of dropping in on Wini. My initial attempt to raise the blinds and let some light into the room was greeted by shrieks of resentment. Thenceforward we sat in the gloom, while Wini moaned into my ears all the miseries of her life, starting from the premise of her having been the youngest of six sisters. I was only required to make murmuring noises in response, which was just as well, because I was puzzled by the whining outpourings of so many ill-defined disappointments. Seeking enlightenment, I asked: "You must, surely, have *some* happy memories?" To which

Wini replied, with emphasised conviction: "Not a single one." The fate of Dorothy and Wini left a lasting impression on my mind.

Horatia Seymour was a completely different kettle of fish. She had a high-bred resilience to the hammer blows of Fate. She would have given a stirring performance on the scaffold, during a revolution. She had beauty and brains and got on very well with men. She had been credited with a lover in youth, but she told me herself that an unmarried girl of her era was afraid to have sexual intercourse with a man, for fear of becoming pregnant, which would have meant social annihilation. Horatia was poverty-stricken all her life. I believe that my mother was instrumental in arranging a whip-round among Horatia's many friends to set up a small trust fund in her favour. She was a cousin by marriage of Mrs Winston Churchill's sister, Nelly Romily. For a time Horatia lived in a cottage in the garden at Chartwell. After the 1945 General Election, Horatia was informed that the cottage was needed for a chauffeur. She therefore moved to a lodging house at Brighton.

My mother's version of the event was that Horatia had rashly admitted that, following her life-long political policy, she had voted for the Liberals in that Election that had proved such a set-back to the Conservative cause and to Mr Churchill's self-esteem. When I suggested that to vote against one's principles would be an act of treachery, my mother replied trenchantly: "Not when your welfare depends on it." I particularly admired Horatia's unEdwardian, uncompromising honesty. The Duke of Wellington, asked to perform some civic duty at Southampton, that would entail staying in that city overnight, wrote and asked Horatia to accompany him. She need have no fear for her honour, he assured her, as he had informed the mayor that she was his cousin. Horatia was much displeased. She was quite ready to appear at Southampton, but not to pose as the Duke of Wellington's cousin, let the mayor think what he liked.

What would have prostrated Wini Pennant, only aroused wry amusement in Horatia. Her younger sister had married a man who received a knighthood. She suggested to Horatia that she should spend the weekend with her at the lodging house in Brighton.

Horatia asked the landlady to prepare a bedroom for her sister, Lady Cheetham. The landlady objected that her house was not fit to receive a lady in. It made no difference when Horatia attempted to explain again that Lady Cheetham was her sister and the landlady did not mind sheltering Horatia beneath her roof. It was made clear that, even if Horatia couldn't see it, there was a world of difference between an indigent spinster and a married lady of title. Lady Cheetham had to go to a hotel.

Horatia was not without the Edwardian steel. I recall a discussion with her at a period when Artificial Insemination by Donor, or A.I.D., was being much canvassed in the press. Horatia, in the exhausted voice that went with her deathly pale complexion, expressed the opinion that it all seemed a great waste of time to her. So much simpler to ask a man to perform the service. But what, I asked, about the husband's feelings? Horatia was certain that, if she was the husband, she would much prefer her wife to experience a natural conception than to be impregnated by *a cold syringe*. She managed to introduce into her voice a note of such horror as suggested she was speaking of some deadly instrument of torture. Rallying from the sound of that languid voice uttering these heresies with such potent effect, I blustered: "but Horatia, what if this man proved much more exciting than poor old Tom at home? That could cause problems." Tremendous, impervious shrugs were the only answer.

Horatia ended her days in a lodging house in Tunbridge Wells, one of a terrace of squat undistinguished red brick houses. She sat with her feet up in the cheerless bed-sitter, with all the easy confidence of one receiving guests in some fashionable drawing room. Her languid voice politely begged the landlady to do this or that small service for her. Requests that the woman carried out under the spell that Horatia had always known how to weave, but never took advantage of.

FLORENCE COURT
—AN ULSTER TIME WARP

*T*O PEOPLE ORIENTATED to modern life it is a matter for marvel why families of means in the 18th century should build such vast houses for their own habitation. The answer is that they did not. The conception was of a permanent home for all living generations of the families that built them. The children were indeed huddled together, with their attendants, in no more than two rooms, in dormitory conditions. But unmarried daughters did not attain their own establishments till late in life. The eldest son brought his bride to live, with whatever number of children they might have, under the parental roof; generally being allotted apartments at the opposite end of the house to his parents, so that a semblance of independent living might be sustained.

Owing to slow and uncomfortable carriage travel, guests came for at least a month at a time, bringing their own attendants. Therefore these large mansions, generally built on the site of earlier, less comfortable dwellings, were in essence hotels packed with guests and family suites. These guests, with their own servants and carriages, could lead their own lives and the entire household needed only to meet together for meals and to spend the

47

evening. From memoirs of the period this style of living would appear to have worked well.

But each generation develops a different outlook on life. The habit of clinging to the parental nest continued into the 19th century, though perhaps on not so general a scale, and with an accompanying deterioration in the amity which seems to have prevailed in the 18th. The 19th century was one of change and transition, which made many families very nervous of the wide-spread trends, and anachronistically determined to keep things as they had been, oblivious of the tide of progress flowing over them.

Sir William Cole, a mercenary soldier in the pay of James I, had arrived in Ireland with the English army in 1607. He had raised for this campaign a troop of Horse from his native Devon. They, and his experience as a soldier of fortune, were of use to him in annexing an area of land bordering on Lough Erne, which had hitherto been in the possession of the Macguires. Sir William and his immediate descendants set to with a will to consolidate their position by founding the town of Enniskillen, evading the death traps set by the Macguires and maintaining their own law and order in the name of the King. They lived, probably in great discomfort, in Enniskillen Castle.

At the beginning of the 18th century, Sir William's great grandson John stepped out of the Law of Piracy into the Age of Reason. He must have come to England, for he married Florence, daughter of Sir Bouchier Wrey, of Cornwall. She shared, if not promoted, his interest in the English Renaissance in architecture. On their return to Ulster, John Cole started building, on an eminence, 9 miles from Enniskillen, a Palladian mansion. He named it after his wife: Florence Court. No documents pertaining to the building remain, so we do not know the identity of the craftsman responsible for the exquisite Italian plasterwork which decorates several ceilings and the walls of the magnificent inlaid wood staircase.

John and Florence's son went on the Grand Tour of Europe and added the elegant wings which flank the square central elevation. It would appear that it was about forty years before the house was completed in its entirety, by which time the Coles had become

Earls of Enniskillen and, after their elevation, extremely dull.

The last one of ability was General Sir Lowry Cole, son of the 1st Earl of Enniskillen. He served with distinction in the Peninsular Wars and became Governor of Mauritius and the Cape of Good Hope.

It was not until 1815, when Sir Lowry was rising 43, that he married Lady Frances Harris, daughter of the noted diplomat Earl of Malmesbury, who, as her parents married in 1777 and had no more than four children, is unlikely to have been in her first youth either.

The 2nd Earl of Enniskillen married, aged 37, Jane Casamajor, a woman of Spanish descent, who claimed a varied quantity of royal blood. Among her ancestors she numbered the Kings of Castile and of León. Should that fail to make a sufficient impression, she was prepared to add King James II of Scotland and King Edward I of England to her lineage.

Her surviving three younger sons and one daughter did not marry, and formed a bizarre entourage around their eldest brother, the 3rd Earl, for the whole of their lives. The middle brother, Colonel Henry Arthur Cole, enlisted in the 7th Hussars, but, on his retirement, hurried back to end his days in Florence Court. He found himself at odds with the resident family, but, instead of buying a home of his own, he moved no further than a room at the end of one of the arcades flanking the house. A small room behind housed his soldier servant. Here he lived in determined isolation, except when, of necessity, he joined his brothers, sisters and sister-in-law for silent meals in the dining room dominated by a full-length portrait of William III, in whose honour it had become family ritual to raise their glasses in the Orangemen's toast.

The former Miss Casamajor had died in 1855 and ten years later Lord Enniskillen married the Hon. Mary Emma Brodrick. Being immured at Florence Court in such an intense family atmosphere seems to have soured the second Lady Enniskillen.

Her eldest stepson, Viscount Cole, later 4th Earl, not unnaturally reacted strongly against the weirdness at home and chose, as soon as he was independent of parental orders, to settle in Cheshire, in a house he rented from Lord Delamere of Vale Royal.

Cheshire took him at once to its heart and he was a popular figure in every stratum of society. Unfortunately for his inheritance, he was a confirmed gambler. When his debts became a problem he married a 17-year-old Scottish heiress, Miss Charlotte Baird.

It would seem that his stepmother did not attend the wedding in 1869, because when Lord Cole brought his bride to Florence Court to introduce her to her future home and its inhabitants, Lady Enniskillen enquired at the dinner table regarding her husband's daughter-in-law and mother-to-be of his grandchildren: "Who is that little red-haired thing giggling away?"

The giggler produced nine children in twelve years, at least one of whom was not fathered by her husband.

She was a woman of great firmness of character. The only recorded instance of her meeting with unopposable opposition was in an encounter with an Ulster countryman on her husband's Fermanagh estate. Lady Enniskillen was driving herself in a one-horse carriage when she pulled up with the wish of leaving the vehicle to examine more closely something that had caught her attention in the immediate environment. Her horse was restive and would have galloped off if she had laid down the reins. In this predicament she asked a humble tenant of her husband's, who happened to be passing, to hold the horse's bridle until she returned. He looked at the mettlesome animal and had no hesitation in refusing.

"You are a coward, Bowles," pronounced her ladyship disdainfully, to which she received the unruffled reply: "Troth and I am M'Lady, and little ever I lost by being one."

When, in middle life, the mutual interests of husband and wife waned, Lady Enniskillen successfully invoked a little known law, the 'femina sole', by which a female could regain full control of monetary settlements, provided she lived as a single woman. With what remained of her fortune she went to live in Florence and later, in old age, in Bath. Meantime Lord Enniskillen invoked his happy gift for friendship and, having made his estates over to his eldest son, had no settled home, but spent the year going from house to house, enjoying the hospitality of other people.

There was an extraordinary coincidental element in the love

lives of the wives of the 4th and 5th Earls of Enniskillen. I have mentioned that one of the sons of the red-haired Charlotte was not sired by her husband. The father was one of the Smith Barry clan from County Cork. When the 5th Earl, as Viscount Cole, got engaged in 1907 to Irene Miller-Mundy of Shipley Hall, Derbyshire (my mother's cousin), her anxious family warned her that she would find life at far away Florence Court very tedious. She replied, her vision clouded by love, that she would be perfectly happy just watching John.

After twenty years and four children this occupation did indeed pall in its simplest context, but on a higher level it gave her a taste for mysticism. Just when she might have hit the London Season to present her eldest daughter, Ann, at Court, she relegated that duty, by default, to a sister-in-law, and disappeared, leaving no address other than her bank, and no information regarding her plans.

A great mystery as to her whereabouts and mode of life prevailed for three years. Some thought she might be in India. But why? And what was the reason behind her leaving no address? At the end of three years she blandly reappeared in August and rented a house on the Thames for a month, where she received her children. They were overjoyed at seeing her again and maddeningly asked no questions: she was not, after all, an erring husband! Augusts beside the Thames became an annual occasion. For the other eleven months of the year she vanished. Until, in August 1937, she died of a stroke in one of these Thames-side houses, in the presence of her distressed son and daughters and their friends.

Gradually scraps of information filtered through to be pieced together. It had been the son of the man who had cuckolded her father-in-law who had aroused her interest in contemplative mysticism. No, it seemed doubtful that they had actually been lovers. He was very fond of his wife. He had, though, placed a window to Irene Enniskillen's memory in the parish church at Yeovale in Somerset. Why Yeovale? Did he live there? Nobody knew. She was my godmother and seemed, outwardly, such a prosaic person.

Irene's four children, my Cole cousins, were born too far apart to have a real sense of comradeship: Ann in 1910, Frances at the end of 1914, Kitty in 1919, and Michael, the longed-for heir, in 1922. Frances and I were very close in childhood and young womanhood, there being little more than a year's difference in our ages, so that Ann, without our being aware of it, felt left out. She was small and inclined to dumpiness, but had a pretty face. My father proclaimed that nobody would marry her because she lacked presence. When she got engaged to Jack James, an intelligent but self-centred civil servant who worked at the Admiralty and later became Deputy Master of the Mint, my father announced that Mr James had not the boots of a gentleman. This was ambiguous. Did he mean that, in 18th century parlance, Ann's fiancé was gentleman-like except for his boots, or that his total lack of gentility extended even as far as his footwear? I did not dare to ask him.

When the war came I lost touch with Frances, who joined the ATS and was posted first to Belfast and later to Egypt. She corresponded rarely, if ever, with her family and friends. I transferred my allegiance to Ann and we remained in touch until she died of complications resulting from the long, remorselessly crippling decline induced by Parkinson's Disease. She never complained nor lost her spirit. In her code of conduct to do so would have been despicable.

Ann and Frances had been uneducated, except for the language, by a narrow-minded bigot of a French governess. After Irene Enniskillen's defection and Ann's London début in 1928, Frances was left alone with the governess at Florence Court, seeing little of her father except at meals. The boredom of the life ate into her soul and she became emotionally dependent on Mademoiselle, confiding in nobody else. On coming out she knew almost nobody in England. When asked by contemporaries what her father did she replied that he was a belted earl, a statement that did her no good at all. Indisputably he was possessed of an earldom, but nobility is not a profession.

Frances's father was a farmer. It dominated his whole way of life. Every morning he either took his thumb stick from the stand in the hall and stumped off to the farmyard, or mounted his pony in the stable yard and rode out to look at his crops and superintend the labours of shepherds, stockmen, ploughmen, woodmen and his gamekeeper. The fathers of many girls pursued the same role with consuming interest, but their precise rank in the social hierarchy was not a matter for comment. One suspects Mademoiselle's influence. Similarly, my mother was properly disturbed when her son, John, wrote home in his first term at prep school with the news that 'we have Lord Templemore's son here'.

I have found members of the Commonwealth to be uncommonly attracted by titles, although they would undoubtedly deny it. I remember one occasion when Frances and I had booked a couple of rooms for the night at a hotel in Dunedin, New Zealand. Frances's father had once told her that when her mother and mine, as young women, went about together, my mother, tall and slim, with an innate dignity, swept into every room ahead of her cousin, while Irene, small-boned and petite, pattered in behind her, like a lady-in-waiting. Frances's father, intimidated by my mother's self-confidence, was intrigued by the less flamboyantly elegant figure in her wake. To my secret amusement Frances took this lesson to heart and edged behind me whenever we entered a room. She need not have bothered. While I had inherited my mother's bearing, I was totally deficient in confidence of any sort and in social popularity there was not any contest between us.

For the above reason I arrived first at the reception desk at the hotel in Dunedin. We were escorted upstairs and I was shown into a large, well-appointed bedroom. As I was unpacking, the hotel manager entered in a state of acute embarrassment. An unfortunate mistake had occurred: I had been shown into the bedroom allotted to Lady Frances Cole. He would give every assistance in making the necessary exchange. In the nicest possible way I begged him not to give the matter another thought. I was perfectly satisfied with the room I had got and saw no reason to suppose that Lady Frances was not equally comfortable. Why should she not be? The hotel manager became so distressed, that I feared he might be about to have a fit. I watched him silently, exuding kindly, if mystified concern. He stammered out renewed requests that I should consent to Lady Frances occupying a room that was patently too good for a commoner, however tall and slim. When I had made it quietly clear that I had every intention of claiming squatter's rights, he tottered from the room, a broken man. I went along the passage to see what the room I ought to have been sleeping in was like. It was perfectly adequate for one night, but very small. Shaking with laughter, I told Frances of my experience; but I suspect she was on the manager's side.

Perhaps because Frances eschewed entirely the usual girlish exchange of confidences about boyfriends, I can remember nothing of what degree of rapport we did enjoy, but a diary kept at the time states that I found in Frances an astringent humour and wished for it in Ann, who was sweeter in character.

The youngest sister, Kitty, had tremendous determination and always felt herself to be different in temperament from her sisters and at odds with her family as a whole. She insisted on being sent to school, which gave her a head start over her sisters in worldliness. From school she wrote home that the girl she liked best was well born, but ill bred.

Not content with being very pretty, she set out to arrest attention by dyeing her fair hair a vivid shade of brass and, later, apricot, and wearing the quantity of make-up necessary to be seen from the back of a theatre gallery. My father never saw her, but, with his instinctive feeling for words, I fear "harlot" might have crossed his lips. On the other hand, if Kitty had wanted to, she could have had him eating out of her hand.

She had very strong romantic ideals. In her opinion Englishmen had no idea how to make a woman feel terrific. She was waiting for young Lochinvar to arrive, though preferably in a white Rolls instead of on a white horse. He failed to materialise. She had swains galore.

"Marry me, Kitty, and I'll be walking on air!" she quoted, with wry disdain. 'Why could he not get his feet on the ground en route to the florist to order bushels of roses?'

She finally married a neurotic refugee Pole, who prided himself on understanding women, their whims and their needs. He put Kitty on the pedestal that she felt was waiting for her and continued to dote faithfully. He also had a nervous breakdown and became very difficult and unpredictable. Kitty performed miracles of tact. I witnessed him being very rude to a friend of hers. Kitty lowered her eyes, Madonna-style, and pretended it was not happening. When the tantrum was over, she raised them again and, with a dazzling smile, promoted general conversation. She was avid for life, interested in everything and very good company. When she found she had cancer of the breast she refused treatment, from a horror of being mutilated. In these straits the Pole became, at last, a tower of strength. He had a deep, if simple, religious faith, a feature of which was that heaven is there, waiting for us, filled only with our loved ones. He sat by Kitty until he had thoroughly imbued her with this single aspect of theology, and she died in the serene conviction of a future of the purest bliss.

After her death it became the Pole's sole remaining joy to lead people on pilgrimages to Kitty's grave in a Brighton cemetery. Standing in front of the headstone on which, I thought, Kitty's rank and title loomed rather too large, I was asked what I thought of it.

"Magnificent," I said, "but I must confess it reminds me strongly of a double-bed head."

The widower was delighted. He was so glad that I had noticed. Not everybody did. It was his intention that they should lie together in death just as they had in life.

When the Cole girls and I were growing up, in the 1920s, Florence Court, except that it boasted two bathrooms, had remained unchanged in every other respect to what it had been in the 18th century. No telephone, no electricity, no central heating. Another 18th century custom remained: because of the distance from England, guests stayed for a fortnight at the very least. This irritated Lord Enniskillen unless they were his particular cronies. He complained consistently about the presence of his daughters' friends. One of them, Ambrosine Phillpotts, the actress, in his opinion spoke too loudly. The Cole girls objected that my voice was equally resonant. Their father agreed, but excused me on the plea that I was more decorative.

Ambrosine put the carrying qualities of her voice to good use as an actress, whereas my strident tones have been the bane of my life. Similarly in decorative quality she easily surpassed me in middle age. She also put her snobbish streak to work for her by taking upper class roles. The Phillpotts to whom she owed her birth, she assured me, were different from and superior to other Phillpotts in that they lavished two Ls and two Ts on the spelling of the name. Thrifty Philpots who made do with one of each, or perhaps managed two Ts, were an inferior breed.

What had been known as the Colonel's Room had become, in the 20th century, the Outside Room, and there we were banished to be out of earshot. Here Ambrosine, aged fifteen, performed most of Shakespeare's plays, singlehanded, taking every role herself, every day, and the tedium of watching this *tour de force* returns to me as I write. Our cousins, by nature indolent, seemed quite content to sit quiescent throughout the one-day stands.

Histrionic in character, nature lent a less kind element to her powers of attracting attention. Cramp would afflict her suddenly, completely; generally when we were out of range of the house. One or two of us would run to the stables, harness a pony to a trap and return at a gallop to rescue the stricken Miss Phillpotts.

When our elders lighted their individual candles, set out in silver candlesticks on the table outside the drawing room door, and went to bed, we were in the habit of climbing out of the library window. It was a stealthily exciting performance. To unpin the heavy iron shutter bar from its socket, lower it without a sound into a vertical position, before folding back the tall wooden shutters without a squeak from the hinges, and raising noiselessly the bottom half of the high multiple sashed window, all by the light of a flickering candle, called for a cool head. Then it was down the long avenue to the crossroads beyond the lodge to join the local lads congregated there. Much laughter and jokes were exchanged; with some persuasion one of the boys could be induced to dance an Irish jig. From Billy Ford, who still lives in the area, I heard the only Irishism spoken by an Irishman: "Aah, yer must not be after trusting t'em cat'olics. T'ey'd cut yer t'roat behind yer back."

At the end of the 1920s, to the uninformed the Troubles were what had happened in southern Ireland. Florence Court was near the Border; there were frontier posts, and one was dimly aware that smuggling was part of the picture. That was all.

The crossroads was not our only social venue. There was a dance that was held in the local Orange Hall that we attended by the same stealthy means. The lancers and barn dances performed to the music of a talented fiddler or accordion player made the Hunt Balls and London dances, that we were to attend later, very pallid affairs by comparison, when the time came for us to depart for an evening's entertainment by the door instead of the window.

Word was passed round of a popular dance to be held at Granshah, a considerable distance away on the road to Lough McNeagh. We conceived the plan of hiring a car and taking the stableman, Jim Price, his wife, Sally and brother John to this event. Jim was doubtful, but was talked round by Sally and John. We confided our intentions to Lord Enniskillen's niece, Angela Villiers. Angela, red-haired from a double dose of Baird blood — her parents were first cousins — was in her mid-twenties, intelligent and sophisticated. She spoke to us very sternly. The fact that we would be leaving the house before the Parent went to bed made detection a strong possibility, in which case the two Price brothers would be sacked out of hand with no redress.

Not only did we not listen to her, we hardly heard her. So, on the evening of the escapade, she sat down beside her uncle after dinner and engaged his attention by encouraging him to talk on subjects dear to him, but infinitely tedious to her. The plan went off without a hitch. A good time was had by all, except Angela. We laughed with her about it the next day. Not for one moment did we consider what we owed to her common sense and quiet assistance in spite of our contempt of her advice, or dream of rendering her any gratitude or thanks.

I vividly recall the fear I felt, when staying at Florence Court, alone at night in a large bedroom, possibly separated by the whole width of the house from the occupant of another bedroom, the dimly flickering light of three candles casting eerie shadows on the enclosed gloom of the walls. It was a fear one could not speak of, a force with which to grapple silently. Later I learnt that the room was reputed to be haunted — some old family murder. I do not reckon that an assassin was necessarily involved: anybody could frighten *themselves* to death. In a similar way, guests at Stanway, in

Gloucestershire, a property of Lord Wemyss, were overcome by a sense of dread in their bedrooms, but that was because Cynthia, the daughter of the house, made a point of telling each guest that theirs was the haunted room. . . .

Florence Court was one of the most beautiful and magnificently executed of almost any Palladian house I have ever seen. Of this fact the Cole girls and I were sublimely unaware. It was their home, just as Petworth House was my father's home, but that they differed, other than in the dimensions of the rooms and their number, from the unpretentious houses inhabited by many of our friends, and from the manor house in Leicestershire rented by my father after the sale of Laxton, passed unnoticed by us. I shared with Catherine Morland, the heroine of Jane Austen's *Northanger Abbey*, the notion that old was beautiful. Artistic appreciation had no place in our upbringing. Pictures and furniture were purely functional and a coloured calendar as desirable as a Constable original. A state of intellectual near-ignorance is comfortable and promotes the herd instinct which the majority of human beings need. I find I have unexpectedly educated myself out of participation in the narrow interests of my contemporaries, although not nearly up to the level of the present generation. Go to a NADFAS[1] lecture and discover that the greater proportion of the audience has come to while away an afternoon. Even if they listen to the lecture, the finer points, especially, any errors, will pass over their heads. Cultural trips abroad will be to Florence, because everybody has heard of that ancient city and it is so handy for taking day trips to places like Vicenza, Mantua, Pavia that can easily be 'done', American style, in a few hours.

Lord Enniskillen liked to make his power and opinions felt among his children, three daughters and, youngest of all, a precious boy. At home my brothers and I were pushed into our parents' bedroom in the morning for about ten minutes, before they got up, and were sent down to my mother's sitting room for an hour after tea. At Florence Court, before we entered our teens, we joined our cousins to watch their parents have breakfast in the dining

---

[1] The National Association of Decorative and Fine Art Societies.

room. We children were ranged round the walls of the room on chairs and forbidden to fidget or speak. At home, nothing was demanded of us and, for most of the day, we passed for invisible, and so this notice, these commands, intrigued me. It became a point of honour not to fidget, and the dining table became a point of focus, since parents approached their food with an interest quite opposed to the unthinking, silent mastication of nurses and governesses. Lord Enniskillen was fond of finding fault and his wife had the responsibility of bringing to the cook's notice anything that had failed to please. Ten to one the cook then left. The master of the house would throw the toast across the room, fulminating that it was dry. As it had been carried a great distance along stone passages from the subterranean kitchen, this was a frequent occurrence.

It was the mode of the period for the girls to paint their lips a vivid scarlet, taking particular pains to form a perfect cupid's bow, even when nature had not supplied it. Colourless complexions needed rouge in order that the face should not appear to be all mouth. Lord Enniskillen's comment on such make-up was to exclaim with revulsion: "Look at her! Raddled like a tup!" In his farmyard the young ram had raddle daubed on his chest before being let loose among a flock of ewes. Those ewes who subsequently carried the red raddle stain on their lower back were thus proved to have been served.

When we were older, we sat round the dining room table ourselves on either side of Lord Enniskillen, who was seated in state at the head of the table, in front of a noble sideboard loaded with silver, above which hung, and still hangs, the full-length portrait of William of Orange. Like former generations of the family, we were drilled, on the anniversary of the Battle of the Boyne, into raising our glasses to the portrait and reciting the Orangemen's Toast. So implaccable was Lord Enniskillen that everybody should be word-perfect, that I still remember the toast in its entirety, although much poetry, including Walter de la Mare's 'The Traveller', a great favourite of mine in youth, and one that I repeated to myself for years, now eludes me.

William of Orange may live in the hearts of certain Protestant elements of Ulster and Scotland, but I had a curious insight into his isolation as King of England once when motoring, at nightfall, from Sussex to Twickenham. After crossing the Thames at Kingston I entirely lost my way. I pulled up at a bus stop to ask for directions. A very rough-looking customer stepped forward, said he was going to Twickenham himself, and got into my car. In the darkness I slid my handbag under my seat and prepared, possibly, to meet my Maker.

Meanwhile conversation seemed to be in order. I asked him where he worked? On the permanent maintenance of Hampton Court Palace, was the reply. In that case he could tell me what I had long wished to know: in which room had the banquet given by Queen Beatrix of the Netherlands been held? In the Great Hall.

I was disappointed. The Great Hall is part of the Tudor palace. The whole object of the exercise, I had supposed, was to use once more, for a particularly fitting royal occasion, the palace built for William III. My companion pondered. Would he be the one whom Queen Victoria succeeded? No, I explained, that was William IV. William III had married Mary II.

"Oh," he said loftily, "you mean *Dutch* William."

The observation astonished me. I hazarded whether they had taught him at Hampton Court Palace to call him Dutch William?

"They teach me nothing at Hampton Court Palace", came the uncompromising answer. "I have always called him Dutch William."

I marvelled. Three hundred years later nothing had changed. The man who had 'saved us from popery, knavery, slavery, brass money and wooden shoes and allowed a poor debtor to walk on a Sunday' was *still* a foreigner and an interloper to the bedrock of the English people.

The Coles must always have been a reclusive family. The central block of the house had only six rooms on each of the two upper floors. The second storey housed the day and night nurseries, the schoolroom and the governess's bedroom as well. The staff quarters had been ordered with a prudent view to the segregation of the sexes. Behind the screen of the arcades on either side of the house were the upper yard and the stable yard respectively. The upper yard was for the storage of the bulk necessities for the household. Above the storage area were the bedrooms of the female staff. Above the stalls and loose boxes of the stable yard were the quarters of the grooms and manservants. It suggested at the same time the feudal concept of a series of courtyards for the housing of animals and retainers, and the Italian building pattern of having the stock and storage buildings adjacent to the main house.

In the 20th century the virtue of the female staff was shattered by the butler, Moisley. I remember Moisley as the typical stage butler: impassive, correct, professional; never condescending to be less than the autocrat, even to us children. He must have been born under the sign of Gemini, for he had another personality. He had served with Lord Enniskillen with the North Irish Horse during the Boer War, and as a comrade-in-arms, he enjoyed his employer's total confidence and protection. As fast as Irene Enniskillen engaged maid servants, Moisley got them pregnant, with monotonous regularity. Lady Enniskillen, a woman of marked simplicity of character, felt that if, with the help of her family, she secured the services of an English girl from her native Derbyshire, either Moisley would note the difference or the girl would fight for her honour.

Neither of these suppositions was justified. Lady Enniskillen felt that not only the girl's honour, but her own and that of her family had been placed in jeopardy. She issued an ultimatum that Moisley must go. The two old soldiers put their heads together: Moisley kept his place, but, to satisfy Derbyshire, married the girl.

My mother faced the same problem with her female servants, although in their case no one man was held accountable. The cook and the head housemaid were sisters of our nanny. "Nan", as we called her, had strange and strong views on sexual problems. On the one hand she counselled against walking through the Burlington Arcade, for fear of passing some unsavoury female person or of being the unwilling witness of an iniquitous approach. On the other hand she taught me, at an innocently early age, the principles of self-defence, culled, at second hand, from somebody's army training. Soldiers were taught the maxim, she informed me:

"If you miss with your bayonet, up with your knee."

Her sisters had not got these matters on their minds and failed to notice the pregnancies of the girls under their control until they were well advanced. One kitchen maid had her baby in the house. Nobody had suspected her condition and she had performed her duties till the moment of her labour began.

This recurrent theme was so common that my mother had devised a routine to deal with it. She arranged for the girls to go to an institution where, after their baby was born, they were found employment where they could keep the child with them. It would appear that, more often than not, the parents of the girls disowned them.

There was one happy ending. Two years after having parted with a certain girl in this manner, my mother received a letter from the signalman at the local railway station. He acknowledged paternity and explained that he was now in a position to marry. Unfortunately he had entirely lost touch with what now appeared to be the love of his life, and solicited my mother's aid in tracing her. My mother and the institution set to with a will and, after a great deal of trouble, since two years is a long time in the lives of people who are not in the habit of leaving forwarding addresses, the young mother fell into her signalman's arms.

My grandmother was concerned in the running of a home for fallen women. She did the accounts. When increasing age made this task somewhat onerous for her, her son-in-law, Vincent Yorke, Henry Green's father, a bluff squirarchical figure, offered to do the job for her. Her gratitude was severely curtailed when Uncle Vincent expressed his ironical regret at finding that shoe leather was still one of the major expenses.

Some years after Irene deserted him, Lord Enniskillen married a widow, Mary Syers. He behaved like a young man who has gained possession of a goddess. It was embarrassing for onlookers, since both were in their fifties and, to my generation, appeared well stricken in years. The second Lady Enniskillen clearly enjoyed her new position and was determined to maintain it, even when, after War broke out, everybody else was losing theirs. Florence Court continued in its time warp. A letter to me from Ann describes this anachronism; or shall I call it solecism?

October 1943 . . . I agree to a certain extent with Egghead that
Mary is very tiresome about rationing the amount of guests at F.
Court. She has shut up the Red Room as she says there are not
enough servants to cope; I leave you to judge of the matter and
give you a list of domestics there. The butler, a parlourmaid, a
cook and a kitchen maid, May as housekeeper with 2 girls as
housemaids (Catholics, much to her disgust). If that isn't enough
staff, what is? I may say *we* were the guests who Egghead ousted
out.

Egghead was my mother's bald brother, Ronald Farquhar, and
Aunt Kathleen in the ensuing part of the letter was Lord Enniskillen's sister and the mother of Angela and Helen Villiers.
Sir Jocelyn Gore-Booth of Lissadell, County Sligo, would
appear, with his family, to have endured a far worse War than
anybody in England. The letter continues:

Aunt Kathleen, when applying for a permit to go to Ireland,
didn't make it clear that she only wanted one for a month and
got one for 6 months by mistake, so when she started making
plans to return to England she was told she couldn't leave the
country, much to Mary's horror, and she made it so obvious that
Aunt K. was a burden that the poor old thing went off all alone
to a guest house in Sligo for a few days and from there to
Lissadell, and when Jack brought the Third Sea Lord to F. Court
for two nights, A.K. was banished to the Loch Erne Hotel!
. . . Aunt Kathleen went to stay a night at Lissadell and
reported that all three girls, Biddy, Rosaleen and Gabrielle were
positively pretty!! I am not sure how much faith I put in this.
The two eldest work all day on the land and Gabrielle is her
father's secretary. Aideen is away somewhere being a nursery
governess. They lead very dreary lives, never seeing such a thing
as a young man day in day out. But what is far worse, I think, is
that there is such a shortage of coal in the Free State that the little
they get goes on the kitchen range and there is none left for the
kitchen boiler, with the result that none of the Gore-Booths
have had a bath for *two years*!

The great sadness for the Cole family as a whole and Michael in particular was that, owing to an accident in school, he had become an epileptic. He was naturally reluctant to mix socially for fear of having a fit.

Staying at the Old Hall, Market Overton, with a cousin of my mother's in the late 1940s, I met that original character, Sir Shane Leslie, a cousin of Winston Churchill. Their mothers had been two of the American Jerome sisters. His home was at Glaslough in County Monahan, the adjacent county to Fermanagh. He questioned me closely about the Coles in general and Michael in particular. I gave it as my opinion that Michael was unlikely to marry, but had the comfort of a steady girlfriend, rather older than himself, a Mrs Pussy Wood.

"Ah," remarked Sir Shane, knowledgeably, "everybody has pussied with Mrs Pussy Wood."

His views were definite and expressed with decision.

"Only Olive," he observed of our hostess, "would live in a house called the Old Hall, that is neither old nor a hall."

Having delivered himself of this statement, he took off his jacket and sat on the floor at my feet. "Scratch my back," he ordered, in front of the assembled company. I was half paralysed with shyness, but it is difficult to refuse a direct command. I scratched his back. Sir Shane, like a cat, gave voice to purrs of pleasure.

In the 1960s Fate struck at the Coles and beautiful Florence Court with a series of tragic blows, Grecian in their relentlessness. Michael died as a result of a fall. A wind of hurricane force blew down the finest trees in the Pleasure Grounds, which made such a superb setting for the house. And lastly, after Lord Enniskillen had reluctantly agreed to install electricity, the house was burnt down, as a result of faulty wiring.

After three centuries the Macguires may be said to have wreaked their revenge.

CHANGING VALUES

*F*ROM TIME IMMEMORIAL, wives in western civili-
sation have been permitted the same licence to have extra-
marital relationships as their husbands, with the
proviso that they should wait till they have performed their
primary duty of giving birth to the all-important son and heir. A
second tacit agreement used to be that on neither side should
embarrassment be caused to the marriage partners of both partici-
pants, and that the concubine had no rights under the law. The
modern readjustment in this unwritten code does not appear, in
fact, to make the people concerned any happier. Both a sense of
dignity, and consideration for the person in the background who is
indirectly concerned, have been casualties.

Working class women will endure anything and everything to
keep their homes together. Upper class women, born into an
environment where only their brothers count for anything, learn
an inbred humility that stands them in good stead in the battle of
life. They know the necessity to be pleasing and how to endure
when pleasing is not enough.

The 8th Duke of Devonshire, known before his father died as
Harty-Tarty (a corruption of his courtesy title of Hartington) was,

over a period of years, accustomed to visit his mistress (eventually his wife) daily at teatime. Harty-Tarty then became an *habitué* of Skittles' establishment and his mistress, the estranged wife of the Duke of Manchester, saw him no more. A year passed, during which the Duchess of Manchester held her head high, concealed her sore heart, and carried on as usual. On the departure of Skittles for Paris, Harty-Tarty appeared once more upon the Duchess's doorstep at teatime as if there had been no interregnum. His mistress took her lead from him, only marking the occasion obliquely by pausing, with his teacup in one hand, the sugar tongs poised in the other:

"It *is* two lumps, isn't it?" she murmured.

Lack of self-respect? Being a doormat? Possibly, but those are two terms unknown in the language of love. The Double Duchess, as Society dubbed her when, after her first husband's death, she married the reformed and renamed Duke of Devonshire, was German by birth, and haughty in spirit, but she loved the second Duke in her life and was prepared to suffer for what she knew was worthwhile, and could not be found in any other relationship.

I recall relating to a kind-hearted but incorrigible womaniser a similar story about Lady Anglesey, an elder sister of Lady Diana Cooper. Lord Anglesey, after some twenty years of married life, got bored and left home. Lady Anglesey, knowing him well, felt convinced that if she behaved herself, he would return. She gave orders to her butler that no gentleman should be admitted to her house after eight o'clock at night.

Two years passed without his wife hearing a word from Lord Anglesey. Then, one evening at ten o'clock, her butler approached and reported that a gentleman was waiting in the hall to see her.

"You know my orders," she objected, "why did you let him in?"

"He is," announced the butler, "the gentleman represented in the photograph beside your ladyship's chair."

Lady Anglesey rose, left the drawing room, and leaned over the banisters.

"Hello Charlie," she said. "Come on up!"

They resumed their married life from there, in great happiness, and she never made any enquiry whatever concerning the last, and for her lost, two years.

I thought this a good story, but was not prepared for the effect it had on my companion. Tears of genuine emotion welled up in his eyes and he exclaimed:

"God, what a woman!"

The Anglesey syndrome might be said to represent, in the eyes of some men, the ideal wife. Whether or not he takes advantage of the opportunity that is open, such a woman will eventually arouse a homing instinct in her man.

John Wilmot, Earl of Rochester, the rakehell poet, who died an early death due to orgiastic over-indulgence at the court of Charles II, left his wife, born Henrietta Malet, much alone at historic Woodstock Manor, haunted by the shades of so many Plantagenet wives and mistresses. Lord Rochester came home to die, and was moved to express the other side of the story in a poem entitled 'Return'.

Absent from thee, I languish still;
Then ask me not, When I return?
The straying fool 'twill plainly kill
To wish all day, all night to mourn.

Dear, from thine arms then let me fly,
That my fantastic mind may prove
The torments it deserves to try,
That tears my fix'd heart from my love.

When, wearied with a world of woe,
To thy safe bosom I retire,
Where love and peace and truth does flow,
May I contented there expire!

Lest, once more wandering from that heaven,
I fall on some base heart unblest;
Faithless to thee, false, unforgiven —
And lose my everlasting rest.

Plas Newydd, the Angleseys' home on that island, remains a shrine of 1920's decor. The main bedroom and bathroom are the work of Syrie Maugham, daughter of Dr Barnado, and wife of Somerset Maugham, who, as the first 'society decorator', started the fashion for all-white drawing rooms; celadon green having previously been the accepted safe colour, not likely to be mocked by sardonic friends. The dining room walls were covered with murals by Rex Whistler with a magical evocation of fairy castles and sunlit seas. In one corner the artist as a handsome yokel is depicted sweeping up leaves. Pride held no place among the Angleseys. The impulse of the moment was given full play.

The Angleseys' eldest daughter, Caroline Paget, a girl of great beauty, became engaged to Lord Knebworth, who was killed in a flying accident. He was a man of exceptional charm and great promise. Lady Caroline did not replace him in her heart by marrying anyone else. In middle life she conceived a child by Anthony Eden. She was too well-bred to think of ruining his career, then at its height. In this plight the Angleseys' neighbour across the Menai Straits, Sir Michael Duff of Vaynol, offered to marry her, on purely platonic terms, to give her child a name. What seemed an ideal solution, offered in kindness, and accepted with gratitude, proved difficult to reconcile for the child. He was potentially the son of Sir Michael Duff but, since he was not of Duff blood, he was not in line for the baronetcy.

The same problem, creating the same unforeseen problems in acceptance, arose when my aunt Violet, wife of the 3rd Lord Leconfield, adopted a girl and then a boy. The boy claimed that, until he grew up, he had no idea that he would not succeed to his putative father's title and estates. His foster cousins horridly aver that, in the nursery, they took every opportunity to keep him informed of the fact. The girl, with the kindest heart and a very good brain, awarded herself false titles which made it impossible for her to maintain a lasting relationship with anyone in the class in which she was brought up, who found these pretensions ridiculous and absurd, and said so.

To this day strange wisps of tales drift around, from time to time, of an unfortunate young lord done out of his inheritance.

My grandfather, Henry Leconfield, had not married till the age of thirty-six, when his bride, Constance, was twenty-one. He at once informed her, as she related to me, that if, after his death, anyone should appear claiming a prior right to the title, his claim should be discounted, since though Henry admitted having had a bastard son, he had seen to it that that son entered the Catholic priesthood, which would preclude him from producing any legitimate heirs.

One cannot absolve those who appear to be in a strong social position from holding very silly notions on the subject of titles. Constance, Lady Leconfield's brother was Archibald Primrose, Earl of Rosebery, who, during his short tenure of the premiership, offered his brother-in-law an earldom. To his credit, Henry Leconfield laughingly declined it on the reasonable excuse that he had done nothing to deserve one. Lord Rosebery was severely critical of his brother-in-law's levity of outlook. He explained that even if Lord Leconfield had no wish to go up in the world himself, he should agree to do so for the benefit of his daughters who, as Ladies instead of mere Honourables, would then be in a position to make better marriages.

One hopes the Prime Minister knew more about politics than he did about his sister's husband, who did not even know his daughters by sight....

Constance, in the company of her youngest daughter Maggie, was entertaining a female visitor when her husband came into the room. Mischievously, his wife said: "Is not Mrs So-and-So's daughter a sweet child?" "Charming, charming," said Lord Leconfield, patting what he did not recognise as his own daughter on the head.

With this sort of start Maggie should have been in a strong position to equal the patient aplomb of the Duchess of Manchester and Lady Anglesey. In fact she played safe and chose not to marry. She was of a neurotic disposition and the thoughtless jibes of her six brothers may have had something to do with it. They told how their sister had had three ardent suitors, the third of whom was so despairing that he had shot himself. Incredulous questioning on our part led to the unromantic *denouement* of the drama: His debts and the fact that his last chance of being able to pay them had gone, had led to the desperate deed.

Her next elder sister Maud was proof against ribaldry. She became the unlikely mother of the novelist, Henry Green, whose works puzzled her not a little. Throughout her life she maintained her own unclouded view of life as an operetta. When I told her of my intention to sail on a windjammer from Belfast to Abo in Finland, I was startled by her mental picture of what the experience would be like.

"My dear," she enthused, beaming, "how delightful; you will valse on the poop deck with the officers!"

From her I learnt that my great Uncle Percy Wyndham had to be allowed to do what he liked, of his great charm and the anxiety he sometimes caused in the heart of his wife, Madeline. Trying, in deep ignorance, to take my aunt's rosy view, I suggested consolingly that perhaps Aunt Madeline had had her lovers too. It was evident that the notion appalled Aunt Maud.

"I am sure she didn't," I said with great conviction, and we were sailing over calm, sunlit seas again, valsing with the officers.

Aunt Maud had hidden depths. When her best loved eldest son fell fatally ill of a lingering illness, she nursed him herself: tirelessly, uncomplainingly, and with complete dedication.

In old age, Maud and Maggie lived in different parts of London. After World War II, when taxis were almost unobtainable, the question arose as to how Aunt Maud was to venture out to dine with Aunt Maggie in safety. I mentioned their problem to my brother John, who observed: "The notion of Aunt Maud being deflowered in the Bayswater Road is an intriguing one."

I returned to question Aunt Maggie discreetly on whether she and her sister were apprehending such a fate. She was openly informative on the delicate subject.

"You may not be aware," she told me, "that youths will often *nudge* one. It is most unpleasant."

Finally an answer to the problem was devised. Aunt Maud's faithful housekeeper, Mabel, would venture out boldly, after dark, to escort her home. My question: "But what if Mabel gets nudged?" was not considered worthy of an answer.

BROUGHT UP AND BROUGHT OUT

*I*N 1923 MY FATHER gave up the plan to found a dynastic homestead, and sold lovely Laxton. I remember standing at the door with my hand on the lintel, waiting to drive away for ever and swearing to myself that I would never love another house. And I never have.

We moved from there to a rented house at Edmondthorpe, near Melton Mowbray.

Life at Edmondthorpe covered that trying period, adolescence. The unvarying, boring monotony of the days has been well expressed by Nancy Mitford in *The Pursuit of Love*. The parents had their own interests and it did not enter their heads to include their children in any of them and thus ease our eventual emergence into grown-up life. We were brought up classlessly: playing with the head groom's three children, Stan, Sid and Elsie. Sometimes the village children joined us, but not that often. Was it the park wall operating again? These playmates were much more inventive than we in thinking up diversions, such as building tree houses, robbing orchards, knowing where birds nested, etc. But they left school and went to work at fourteen.

The mid-teens were the boring period. Lessons were made so

dull that I did not even try to learn. Brenda Alexander's father was in command of the Remount Depot at Melton Mowbray. She lived with her parents at Whissendine, five miles from Edmond-thorpe. when two French governesses, one Papist and one Huguenot, had left after twelve months each of coping with trying to teach me French and the piano, and not being recognised, either by my parents or by the domestic staff, as being the *bien* characters of Gallic distinction that they considered themselves to be, my parents and Brenda's got together and decided to combine forces and wages by employing a shared governess, who would live under the Alexanders' roof and teach us two girls, who were, at that time, twelve years old.

A Scottish lass, Miss Murdoch was engaged. We called her 'Murky' and, in no time, had sussed out her weaknesses. Unlike Calvin, she was pitifully unaware of evil, especially when mani-fested in the form of two innocent young girls. In connection with a history lesson, let us say, one of us would earnestly ask what that word, *adultery*, upon the printed page, meant. From there we took it in turns to be relentlessly anxious to seek enlightenment.

"Making love to another man's wife? But why? I mean, if a man has a wife, what would he be doing with somebody else's wife that he couldn't do with his own?"

"Yes, Murky — I mean, Miss Murdoch — it is important that we should understand, else how can we write our compositions? Brenda, do *you* understand what Miss Murdoch means?"

"No, I don't. Please Murky, how is adultery different from what a husband does with a wife? Or don't you know?"

As with the French governesses, Miss Murdoch held out for a year against onslaughts on various aspects of a subject that she considered taboo. She then, in tears, informed Mrs Alexander that she could no longer put up with what she termed our consummate insolence. We thought that we had seen and heard that word and that it was spelt and pronounced consum*a*te. Didn't that just show how ignorant Murky was? Mrs Alexander was too annoyed to reply.

The end of the governess era meant that Brenda was sent to

boarding school and I to a day school in Queen's Gardens in London. I was to live, during the week, with my grandmother, in Stanhope Gate, where my father was already a weekly boarder. My mother liked to have a certain manipulation over her children's friendships, and a day school was cheaper than a boarding school. I was every bit as horrified at the idea as though I was about to be transported to Australia. I prayed desperately for an act of God to deliver me from this terrifying fate.

For the next three years I learnt absolutely nothing, except a faint interest in English literary style. This subject was well taught by Miss Faunce, the Principal, who like Queen Victoria, was almost as broad as she was long, and had practised queenly dignity. She did not come into a room, she made her entrance. She would not have considered John Brown as an escort unless he could have proved at least sixteen quarterings. The reiterated injunction to remember that we were ladies, carried with it so many tedious restrictions that I forsook it, there and then, and have been a woman ever since.

Her staff consisted of several dispirited, ill-favoured females, who were earning their living because they had to. They were totally uninterested in the irksome profession that a merciless fate had forced on them. Rosamund Hornby made it her business to divert them from the subject they were supposed to be teaching onto any other. When, rather later than sooner, they dimly realised that they were not acting according to the book, Rosamund chipped in again with: "But it's so *interesting. Do* tell us a little more." They then, with faintly rising animation, meandered off the subject once more. Personally, I found the reflections of unimaginative, untalented women just as tedious as the ungarnished information contained in the text books lying open on our desks.

When I was fifteen I, and the daughters of three of my mother's friends, were sent for confirmation classes to a fashionable clergyman: the vicar of Putney. Mary Crewe-Milnes, Mary Ormsby-Gore, Betty Coates and I gathered weekly in Putney for instruction. I, for one, had several points that I wanted clarifying. Why was it so necessary to look upon Jesus Christ as God. It was as a human being that one could identify with Him, gain some insight into the basic fact that, in suffering, none of us is alone. As a human being He had suffered all the earthly torments that beset mankind; hopefully with the same sense of insecurity, of hopelessness, and of fear that is peculiarly human. There is a necessarily uncertain, unprovable element to faith which, as God, Christ would not have had to wrestle with as He grappled with loneliness, desertion, temptation, misunderstanding, humiliation, followed by a death of unimaginable agony. During which, to my incomprehension, He called upon what was Himself, asking why He had been forgotten.

Lacking interest in my lessons, I had inherited my father's curiosity with regard to imponderables. He read widely in philosophy and theology, searching, with increasing disappointment, for a reassurance as to his own rightness and importance in the narrow confines of personal existence.

Another comfort in favour of Jesus being entirely human was His endearing need for small personal attentions, lovingly bestowed; to the extent of wishing, once in a while, to forget the poor, who would be always out there, needing help, whereas His time was short and heavenly bliss a somewhat uncertain future. Could the Three-in-One concept, including another incomprehensible mystical ghostly emanation, be a carry-over from the long-held multi-deism of all primitive religions?

Pontius Pilate was more responsive than the fashionable vicar. He skirted my questions as an interruption and continued with his sermonising. None of my companions cared either way. It was not till five years later, when Mary Crewe-Milnes got engaged to a duke and received a demand from the fashionable vicar that he should conduct her fashionable wedding service, in Westminster Abbey, that she wholeheartedly shared my opinion of this man — viewing him from the opposite end of the spectrum.

At the age of sixteen, I was sent to a finishing school at Versailles, where the class barrier was encountered for the first time. In the small society of the day it was possible to tell from a girl's name who her father was, where he lived, what he did. It was likely that one had a friend or relation in common. A facile short cut to amicable intimacy was thus established. If the name of anybody did not ring such a bell, they were outsiders. Not one of these outsiders had the gumption to pretend her father was something unusual like, for instance, an acrobat. By so doing she would have excited the keenest envy in the hearts of all her companions. To stand out from the crowd was the unspoken aim, as indeed it is today.

I invented a half-wit sister, called Hyacinth, shut away in some home for harmless loonies, because her presence would have been an embarrassment to the family. I was disconcerted that this, to me, unlikely story was accepted as better than likely, as Mr Brontë would have put it, and a torrent of interested questions, all sympathetic to Hyacinth, and for which I had not devised the answers, rained upon my guilty head. In those days the disadvantaged were at least individual in their disabilities. They were idiots or lame or blind. Nowadays they are lumped together as mentally, physically or visually handicapped. Handicap = the same unvaried umbrella under which all sufferers are forced to shelter. Calling a spade a spade is more honest and more challenging to accept than to reissue the term under the obscure title of garden operative's implement.

It is possible that, subconsciously, I identified with Hyacinth. I told myself, in my early teens, that the importance attached to the words 'affection' and 'love' was silly. All one required in life were clothes to keep one warm and food to keep one going. None the less although, in these reflections, I had ignored the needs of the spirit, when my mother arranged *matinée* visits to the theatre, in company with Helen Villiers, who had a governess to chaperone us, I intuitively decided that these treats had an ulterior motive. They were to salve her conscience for her inability to feel any affection for me, or to involve herself personally in the development of my mind and how to gain an understanding of myself in the framework of human responses. It was a pity that I came to that conclusion, because it took the edge off my enjoyment of the ventures.

The Versailles finishing school was like a prison. The grounds were surrounded by chain-link fencing, eight feet high, and the

entrance gates were kept locked. Two of my fellow pupils committed suicide a few years later. Mary Peel shot herself, which is a very
unusual method for a woman to choose to put an end to her life.
She was beautiful, kindly, warm-hearted and deeply religious. To
this day nobody knows why she committed the mortal sin of
self-destruction.

The other girl, Judy Muir, whom I also found congenial, was
red-haired, with thick ankles. She jumped off the roof of her home
in Gloucestershire. She could be amusing, in the sense of having a
fine vein of irony, which may have disguised unhappiness. As
Byron wrote: 'And if I laugh 'tis that I may not weep.'

I had to write home in order to get permission to read André
Maurois' biography of the poet. I also had to write home to explain
that my father's teaching was about to get me expelled...

My father preached nudism. There was nothing evil about the
body, he averred, but thinking made it so. He was able totally to
disconnect nakedness from sensuality, while in no way admitting,
far less explaining to a daughter who was very conscious of her
body, that one can be a part of the other.

I had walked from my bedroom to the lavatory, in a house
containing no one but females, naked. Unfortunately I met
Mademoiselle Fauchet, the Principal, in the course of this short
peregrination. There was so much loud disquisitioning from
Mademoiselle, in which the word "sauvage" was the main refrain,
that every door opened on what I had hoped would be a private
expedition.

My parents, incomprehensibly astonished at what seemed my
irrational fear of them, sent me to a psychoanalyst. My maiden
aunt Maggie, of all people, wrote to the woman, informing her of
my early introduction to the naked male. The news was received
with electrifying excitement by my analyst. What could I
remember of my father's genital organs? Nothing. I truthfully told
her. Ha! So I had repressed all recollection of them! I replied that I
did not feel that I had; I equally could not recall the shape of his
arms and legs, nor how muscular his chest was. This information
was rejected out of hand and only the genitalia were allowed on
stage.

*Me, aged 22 months with my mother
and a large dog.*

*Petworth (by kind permission of the
National Trust)*

Florence Court

Christmas at Petworth, 1922. From left to right: my mother and father, my Aunt Violet and my Uncle Hugh. Sitting in front of the fire, my Uncle Humphrey, and to the right of the fireplace, my Aunt Maud, my Grandmother, Constance Leconfield, my Aunt Ruth and Uncle Charles, Lord Leconfield.

At Florence Court. Frances Cole, Henry, myself, Anne Cole and Kitty Cole.

Me in 1932

*Lord Enniskillen claimed I looked like Queen
Nefertiti and wanted a photograph to prove it.*

*My father, out hunting with Sir Raymond Greene
and Lady Manton.*

Mark, me and John. I am dressed for hunting.

From 'The Bystander', July 1935. Frances Cole
and I on the 'Herzogin Cecile'.

Aunt Maud and I in Venice, 1935. Note that I am wearing the clothes that I would wear in London which while usual then seem ridiculous for a tourist.

Rags and me, 1935.

In Pretoria, mid-1980s.

The next act was even more bewildering. What did I know of sexual feelings? I explained that I had never experienced any. This, it appeared, was bad and must be remedied. I asked what was the point of inducing sexual feelings when there was nobody around who had expressed a desire to gratify them? I suppressed, in this unsympathetic climate, the information that the only emotion I deeply feared and would not know how to cope with was unrequited love, and, with this in mind, snubbed any advances from the opposite sex.

I was interrogated as to my emotions towards my own sex. I had to confess to a complete lack of interest in that area also, even when at school. It was becoming increasingly obvious that, as in my relations with my parents, I was not giving satisfaction in the psychological field either. The order was given that, in conjunction with pills, I must induce these dormant sexual feelings by rubbing my body in its most susceptible parts. I was deeply shocked. I had heard of this practice. I even knew its name: masturbation—and it had been represented as Not a Good Thing.

I obeyed orders. What else could I do? I found the performance ineffably boring and it had no effect at all. However, no experience need be a waste of time, and mine, at the hands of a well-meaning psychoanalyst, laid the foundation in my mind, which took several more years to surface, that I must begin to think for myself, to develop my intuitive instincts and cease to live in the shadow of my parents — who had a deep respect for the ancient Greek precept of exposing unwanted babies on the hillside, and wondered how such an excellent custom had come to fall into disuse and distrusted psycho-analysis that went by the book and took insufficient accounts of the basic fact that human beings are individuals and do not, necessarily, react to identical pressures in the same way.

It was at Versailles, aged sixteen, that I read Axel Munthe's *Story of San Michele* and learnt, for the first time, that the emotions of men and women are very different. It was a disturbing discovery, leading to several lone walks round the inner perimeter of the chain link fence, to arrive at a condition of acceptance.

Some of us were escorted to a performance of *Cyrano de Bergerac*. What a seductively persuasive language French is! Hearing an

English translation on the wireless left me unmoved. Similarly, to receive the full rapturous horror, *Les Liaisons Dangéreuses* must be read in French.

Growing up in the Edwardian era, one could not but be aware that it was an intensely materialistic age. One felt the steely values in one's own parents: the father who had but one answer to any of his children's dreams and plans — 'Don't expect any help from *me*'; the mother's golden advice — 'Always get things the way you want them while your husband is in love with you; if you don't do it then, you never will'.

Stories abound. Mrs Keppel, in the evening of her life, was entertaining a lunch party at her villa in Florence. A very nervous American girl, rocking backwards in her chair, broke it. That, as I was told it, was of no account: the chair cannot have been worth more than £200[1]; but, in her struggles to regain her balance, the girl lashed out with her arms and displaced a priceless Chinese porcelain figurine, that shattered on the floor. Her plight was terrible, as Mrs Keppel's icy rage knew no mercy.

My mother was fond of telling of the woman who had been given a gold box by an admirer. Something about it left her dissatisfied and she took it to be valued. It weighed in at only fifteen carats, so the contemptuous recipient threw it away.

It was an era when almost every man had a nickname, as though nobody wished to see his comrade as he was, but as the mind of the beholder recreated him: 'Boguey', 'Methuselah', 'Scatters', 'Tops', 'Troops', and, so supreme they must be given in full, 'Creepy' and 'Crawley' de Crespigny.

The letters of Raymond Asquith at that time give a tantalising glimpse of a young man of great charm and wit, deeply clever, deeply perceptive, deeply cynical, deeply disillusioned, shallowly despairing of finding any meaning to life, of a way through the wood of a repetitive society. Younger sons were emigrating to Kenya, professing themselves to be bored and unfulfilled by the empty frivolity of existence in England — and then setting up precisely the same style of life in East Africa.

---

[1] Multiply by 10 for present-day values.

Perhaps the Prince of Wales' Pied Piper tactics of leading Society on an endless merry-go-round of gambling, scandal, cover-ups, lies, and gossip — the constant chance of the unexpected, personified by Lord Charles Beresford leaping, with a hearty cry of "Cock-a-doodle-do!" into what is variously reported as the bed of the Bishop of Chester (or was it the Bishop of Oxford?) because he had mistaken the location of the bedroom of the woman he had allotted to himself for that night — really did add up in the minds of all but a few nonconformists to a satisfying *modus vivendi*. Sooner or later a splinter group was bound to hive off, and the 'Souls', while maintaining the sexual freedom which had been part of the Prince's piper's tune, developed the arts of the intellect — which those like Raymond Asquith suspected was not quite sufficient to offer at the bar of Heaven, in which he did not believe, as proof of a full and satisfying life.

The Edwardians prided themselves on knowing precisely who had fathered every woman's child, and naming the father whenever the person in question was mentioned. This masquerade was conducted against a background of the Irish question, Keir Hardie's aspirations, the Boer War, and tension in Europe. What was there to cling to in a changing pattern but the material aspects of life, more especially as they seemed to be slipping away?

The still prevailing gloating love of underlining scandal in Edwardian times was the means of me discovering early in life from the Coles (whose own parents had, of course, mentioned the fact, although the cover-up element had precluded them from being in possession of any details) that my maternal grandfather had had to flee the country to avoid a prison sentence.

This was fascinating news, made all the more wonderful in that judicious questioning revealed the undoubted fact that neither my mother nor her brother knew anything of the matter. We were all amazed at parental obtuseness. We would know, we told each other, if *our* parents got up to any tricks.

Finding out was one of the highlights of childhood confabulations and consultations with contemporaries. We all had a keen academic interest in sex, but it was much more fun to argue, debate, get the idea all wrong and then, subsequently, be in a position to amend previously held opinions, than to question parents or nannies, as we were encouraged to do, which would have turned the whole fascinating concept into just another dreary lesson. But the exact nature of my grandfather's crime eluded us forever. Frances Cole was deputed to ask her father for enlightenment. The answer, in the first instance, was encouraging: "There is only one person who could tell you that." Questioned eagerly as to the identity of this key witness, his next answer, delivered with the taciturnity that parents used in communication with their offspring in those mid-1920s days, was: "He died ten years ago."

THE COUNTRY
HOUSE VISIT

WHEN STAYING in large houses in winter, one had the pleasure of a fire in one's bedroom, from six o'clock in the evenings onward. There are few simple pleasures equal to lying snugly in a large bed watching the flickering shadows of the firelight on the ceiling. It was as delightfully soothing as the dim glimmer of candlelight was frightening. Like all pleasures it had to be paid for. In the icy morning one had to rise and hustle quickly into one's clothes with nothing but the cold embers for company. This was before the age of charwomen and the housemaids were busy setting to rights the many rooms on the ground floor that had been in use during the previous day.

In the daytime, the men and women sat in separate rooms: the host had his business room and the hostess her sitting room, where they could go to write letters or just have a breathing spell away from the house party. There was the room in which the party assembled before lunch and another one in which they assembled before dinner. After dinner the company adjourned to one of the largest rooms in the house to play a variety of games.

A nervous young male guest, unaware that the room in which a large houseparty assembled after dinner was not in use on a daily basis, asked his host: "Is this your chair?" before presuming to sit on it. The reply "All the chairs are mine" was not enlightening.

The butler and footmen who stood behind the dining room chairs during lunch and dinner overheard social secrets and political scandals that today would make them a fortune from sales to the press. There is no reason to suppose that they ever repeated these titillating conversations to anybody. Their discretion was taken absolutely for granted. When one reflects on the remorseless pressure put by reporters on the royal family today, even when they are off duty, so to speak, and on holiday, and compares it with the discretion exercised by the British media regarding King Edward VIII's relationship with Mrs Simpson during the last five years of his career as Prince of Wales, it is as though surveying life upon a different planet.

Mrs Simpson, never haughty before her marriage, and never less than demanding after it, lost the chance of a lifetime by not having the acumen and intelligence to realise that, by refusing to marry the King and insisting that he remain on the throne, she could have become a formidable source of hidden power, since she ruled him completely until the day he died.

It was said the Prince of Wales knew that he was incapable of siring children and thus had no inducement to make a dynastic marriage. None of his previous female favourites had exerted any lasting influence over his whims. Mrs Simpson's success in this area was therefore inferred to be attributed to the theory that she was the only woman who was capable of giving him the sexual satisfaction on a level that he had failed to find in any of his many other relationships. This theory developed in the telling to the degree that the Prince was reputed to be near to impotent. One of his most loyal loves has recently put on record that there was nothing inadequate about the Prince's sexual performance. It none the less remains a feasible assumption that in this area lay the basis of Mrs Simpson's remarkable ascendancy.

The new favourite was welcomed by the Prince's friends. She fitted in. Like them, she considered that the height of human pleasure to be experienced sprang from having a wide choice of cocktails to drink and of games to play: Backgammon—a game that has been satisfying hedonists for thousands of years — Bezique, Bridge, Poker and, of course, as with Backgammon, Sex. Mrs Simpson excelled at all of them and also at the fairly obvious one-liners that passed for wit. An example of these — that one should always try everything twice; except incest and Morris Dancing — has had a miraculous resurrection after forty years. It may be that this life was the summit of her ambition and that the power to manipulate her Creature on a national, or possibly even international level, was one that called for a degree of concentration which would either have bored her or been beyond her imagination. Whatever the reason, in the area of feminine calculation, she must rank as a prime misser of opportunities.

It is part of this notorious couple's aura of having no fixed place of abode on two continents that they should have met at Melton Mowbray. The night life to be experienced there was one in which they could readily participate.

The anti-blood sports fanatics take the wrong line in their protests. They are unaware that a bolted fox is given the length of a field start of hounds; that 75% of hunting days do not end in a kill; that there is a closed season for breeding, which would certainly not be adhered to if the fox was designated vermin. What they are also not aware of is that the excitement of the chase makes for a certain randiness among the regular followers.

What also needs to be stated in connection with two aspects of life that are not supposed to have changed since the '20s and '30s, is that the sports of both hunting and polo are now barely recognisable by comparison with what they then were. Recently a friend of mine, who should have known better, enthused that he had met a very interesting man at a dinner party the night before. As interesting people in the provinces are rather thin on the ground, I asked eagerly what this man of parts did with his life. I was informed, in tones of awe, that he 'hunted with the Quorn'.

In the 18th century landowners put a lot of thought and discussion into breeding the right hounds for the terrain over which they were to hunt. Every countryman was involved. There were no class, far less intellectual, barriers. Surtees's endearing tales of the grocer, Mr Jorrocks, carry on the tradition. When I hunted at Melton one of the most respected followers was a tramp-like figure who, by reason of his deep knowledge of natural lore, knew all the foxes intimately and the line individuals would be likely to take. The huntsman was, at times, not ungrateful for his advice. It was humbling, after a tricky run, when one was congratulating oneself on having kept hounds in sight, to find this man also present, having got there on his feet, by taking short cuts dictated by country cunning.

Anybody was welcome in the hunting field as long as they knew the rules — which was where the young fellow from Bristol had slipped up. This footfollower made an income by holding open gates for the mounted followers. Knowing him well, they tipped lavishly. I do not doubt that he did some poaching on the side, to which he owed his woodland instinct. It was the custom to tip those who held open gates. I remember riding home with Bruce Shand on one occasion, who put some coins into the hands of two youths, with the warning: "Now boys, don't go spending this on fast women and slow horses." The recipients gaped.

Another acquaintance, visiting the vast continent and ancient culture of India was only impressed that he happened to fall in with an ex-body servant of the Maharajah of Jaipur, who had followed 'Jai' (as my informant referred to a person he had never met) to the polo ground at Cirencester and had photographs to prove it.

Polo had certainly been played in India for over a thousand years before the era of the British Raj. The British army in India took it up and it became an inter-regimental sport, played in the best traditions of the sporting spirit as a game that called for a true eye and fine horsemanship. One of these players deplored to me that the introduction of paid 'hired assassins' from South America had debased a gentleman's game into a professional sport such as football, with a vast 'gate' that has come not so much to take an interest in the game as to gawp at the royal family.

To return to the Melton Mowbray climate in which Edward and Mrs Simpson were not at home: she had never been on a horse and the Prince did not appear at ease or to advantage in the hunting field. He was no horseman, and increased the insecurity of his seat by riding with very short stirrups and using the reins as a means of support, thus inhibiting his horse from successfully negotiating the possible double oxers and 'bullfinches' (a thick, high, unlaid hedge) which were a hazard of the open Leicestershire country. The Prince had many falls.

Serious hunt followers crammed their hats down on their heads and rode purposefully across country. H.R.H. wore his at the rakish angle that Jack Buchanan and Fred Astaire in his day and Frankie Vaughan and Tommy Steele in ours, have used to establish their style on stage. That was where the Prince of Wales, in his attire, seemed always striving to be, which was at odds with his shy, boyish manner. Woody Allen has now capitalised on this paradoxical characteristic. And, indeed, such wistful dualism established the Prince of Wales' especial charm while, at the same time, making him the prey of a feminine character far stronger and more determined than his own. Alone, in any situation, he exuded an aura of little boy lost.

Lady Diana Cooper, even when Ambassadress in Paris, always flouted the royal order not to curtsey to the Duchess of Windsor, on the grounds of it being a harmless act of courtesy that gave pleasure. This would not have been the interpretation that the Duke desired, had he known of Lady Diana's explanation.

Watching, on television, people being presented to the Queen today, one notices that is is no longer inevitable that every individual will either bow or curtsey. This formality was still unbreakable between the Wars and the rigidity of the principle extended to the Monarch's representatives. Staying, in complete informality, at Government House, Wellington, New Zealand, while the Governor General and all his staff, except one equerry, were away on a fishing trip, I saw no reason to continue to curtsey to my parents' old friend, Lady Galway, after her initial greeting. When the cosy party consisting of myself, Frances Cole, the equerry and Lady Galway's lady-in-waiting parted from her at bedtime, I was about to turn towards my bedroom door, when the lady-in-waiting hissed at me, from between clenched teeth, "Curtsey!". I dropped obediently on one knee. Unlike many of my contemporaries, I had not been taught this accomplishment by a professional instructress, my mother holding that it was cheaper to issue the deceptively simple command: "Get down as low as you can without finding that you cannot get up again, and keep your back straight." That last bit is very difficult.

Hospitality has never been an English characteristic and the uninvited guest was, and I think still is, made to feel just that. You do not see the word 'welcome', even hypothetically, on many mats. It has always been a more complicated matter for those who live in stately homes. Putting the kettle on and then enjoying a mug of tea or coffee across a kitchen table has a snugness that encourages a good exchange of views. It is a cold gulf away from ringing the bell and waiting for the whole paraphernalia of tea-making to be brought in on a silver tray. A case in point occurs to me.

In the mid 1930s Brenda Alexander and I went on a riding tour of the Dukeries, in the Sherwood Forest area, so called from the number of dukes who, at one time, had properties there. By then the number had been sadly depleted, but the Duke of Portland still lived at Welbeck Abbey. He had two daughters with whom I had a nodding acquaintance. We put our horses and ourselves on the train at Melton station and unloaded them at some halt in Nottinghamshire, the name of which I have forgotten.

The adventure, while interesting, proved to be more hazardous than we had supposed. We used our fathers' military saddles which were designed to carry every accoutrement from swords to saddle-bags. Few inns still had accommodation for horses and, at those that had, the straw was cleaner than the sheets. Farms, which could cater to all a horse's needs, were less ready to be at the trouble of housing riders, in those days before the bed and breakfast trade had been thought of. It became almost a re-enactment of the Bethlehem story. In fact we never actually had to sleep in a stable, but at times we feared that fate. We covered about twenty miles a day and the evenings were spent sandpapering the bits of the doubles bridles that started to rust as soon as we took them out of the horses' mouths.

The midday halt had been a foreseen anxiety. The horses wore halters under their bridles, the ropes of which were knotted round their necks. When we stopped, daily, for a picnic lunch, we loosened the girths, removed the bridles so that the horses could graze, but felt obliged to tie the halter ends to a rail, in case they made off. This act naturally restricted their grazing. It was a surprise to discover that the horses were as frightened of losing us as we were of losing them. If we wandered out of sight, they exhibited signs of panic. This discovery was a heart-felt relief. We turned them loose and all four of us were happy and at ease.

I had never been to Welbeck, so, passing the entrance gates, we turned in and rode up the drive to the house. I rang the bell and asked for Lady Anne, with whom I was the better acquainted. The reply came that she was away, so I inquired for her sister, Lady Peggy. Anne rode and hunted. Peggy did neither. She came to the door and, surveying our nomadic appearance, an expression of distaste flitted across her refined features. She was immaculately dressed in the sort of country clothes that one would not expose to much energetic country usage. I began a recital of our ordeals in the hope that Peggy would send for a groom to lead our horses to the stables and invite us to cross the threshold of the Abbey to partake of sherry and biscuits or the like. Her mind worked differently. Some genetic instinct reminded her of the custom of feeding beggars at the gate and she asked, in a tone of fastidious obligation, whether she should call the footman, still waiting in the background, to bring out some sandwiches to us?

My genetic impulse was to have no truck with such a conde-scending idea. Brenda, however, untrammelled by such inhibi-tions, made haste to accept the other, for both of us, before I could refuse it. The sandwiches were presented to us, on a silver salver, where we stood, by our horses heads, at the front door. They were delicious.

As we rode down the drive towards the entrance gates, our stomachs full, Brenda uttered the outside-the-wall observation that she had been determined to get what ducal bounty she could for us, whatever the odds. And they had been considerable.

A much happier instance of hospitality, this time over a weekend, has remained firm in my memory because, during the same period, in 1934, the Royal Navy submarine *Thetis* sank to the seabed and was unable to resurface. Desperate, though in the event unavailing, efforts were made to raise her, while the whole ship's company slowly perished, as their hopes of the possibility of rescue died with them.

My brother, Henry, was much enamoured of Arbell Mackintosh, whose grandmother, Evelyn, Dowager Duchess of Devonshire, lived at Hardwick Hall in Derbyshire. Arbell had no looks, but, what were far more potent, tremendous zest for life, enthusiasm and entirely natural charm. It was kind of her to include me, who was two years older (which was quite a lot in those days, when one associated mainly with those who had come out the same year as oneself), in her invitation to Henry and other contemporaries to spend a June weekend as the guest of 'Grannie Evie'.

I was thrilled. Hardwick is Tudor, both in design and date, and, as such, represented for me all that a house should be in romantic interest and beauty. An extra bonus proved to be the remarkable fact that even the bathroom was hung, on all four walls, with tapestry. As in my bedroom, a slit had been made to enable one to open the door, if one leaned heavily against it from the outside and pulled the heavy hangings aside from the inside. I daresay this was almost as good as central heating to the Elizabethans.

Evie Duchess had the reputation of being intimidating. In spite of my crippling shyness, I did not find her so. She was forthright and one knew exactly where one was with her: a welcome change from the home ground where my father was out to snub my nervous callowness and my mother changed her opinions overnight to suit the social majority view of the moment, and was equally snubbing if one queried the volte-face.

A mystery hung over the scene. Diana Daly, an older woman, graceful, handsome and witty (and grandmother of the officer who was killed in command of the troop of the Household Cavalry who were victims of the bomb outrage in Hyde Park), was ill in bed upstairs. I was curious to know what was wrong with her. Arbell did not know, nor seemed to care. I would have to ask the Duchess. As the case was such a source of mystery I felt that I could only require an explanation in private, and the chances of finding myself alone with our hostess appeared slight. Intensely inquisitive by nature, the matter was developing into an obsession with me.

Meantime, in golden sunshine, we explored the ruins of the Old Hall, and sat in the garden, gazing at the bluest of skies— unable to detach our minds from that trapped company of men in the doomed *Thetis*, news of which came regularly over the wireless.

On Sunday evening, after dinner, when I had lost hope of discovering the nature of Diana Daly's malady, fate came tardily to my rescue. Arbell suddenly suggested exploring the roof. The rest of the company expressed equal enthusiasm. My parents would undoubtedly have vetoed the idea of clambering about the roof in the gathering twilight. Surprisingly, Grannie Evie made no difficulty and hardly looked up from her knitting. I was playing Patience and excused myself from joining the eager company, seeing, as I did, a perfect opportunity for getting in the long-awaited question. Arbell and her friends left the room. I, while putting one card upon another, tried to make my voice casual as I voiced my eager enquiry: "What is wrong with Diana?"

The Duchess's needles continued their steady click.

"Floodings," she informed me — and we each continued with our pastimes.

The Hardwick visit was in mid-summer. A hazard of mid-winter visiting was that, apart from rising and dressing in ice-cold bedrooms, the custom of the day was for wearing full evening dress for dinner. The mode of the moment followed the supposition that the spinal column is a seductive area, and evening dresses were cut down to the waist behind. This precluded the possibility of wearing warm underwear in rooms with high ceilings that the old-fashioned central heating system was incapable of adequately warming. Shivering with cold, and one's brain in an equal state of numbness, one desperately groped for some interesting topic of conversation to get one through dinner, seated between two strangers.

A weekly literary magazine ran a competition for the three best opening gambits for conversation. It was an area in which I felt a perpetual failure, so I entered. I did not win, but I got an honourable mention. The gambit that pleased the judges was: "Have you seen the roasted man at the British Museum?". I had only recently seen him myself and would not have tried out that one in real life, from a near certainty that none of my dinner party partners would have known where the British Museum was located, let alone its more obscure contents.

"Do you prefer pink or blue hydrangeas?" was considered by the judges to drag my entry below the level that deserved a prize. That one I had encountered and, puny though it may be in the light of philosophic argument, the partner of the moment and I had discussed it frantically for five minutes or so.

MAKING HAY
WHILE THE SUN SHONE

DURING THE 1930s mothers were unaccountably frightened that their daughters, unless constantly on the alert, would be abducted by the White Slave Trade. Terrible warnings were dinned into my already overvulnerable ears. I must, on no account, help an old woman across the street. She would have have jabbed me with a hypodermic needle before we reached the traffic island in the middle, while accomplices waited to spring. Twenty-five per cent of the taxis in London were not taxis at all: they had no handles on the inside of the doors, so that, once a girl was in them, she was trapped. Need I say that, precisely at this juncture, a new design in taxis appeared on the street, in which the handle was set unobtrusively into the fabric of the inside of the doors, instead of being, as hitherto, the outstanding type that the hand could grasp. The first time I got into one of these new taxis I virtually had hysterics and screamed to the driver to let me out. He must have thought I was mad, not being disadvantaged enough to have an upper-crust mother.

My grandmother, Constance Leconfield, lived in London at 12 Stanhope Gate. Her house was a hotel for her children and grandchildren. My mother had keen aspirations to be a London hostess. On my *début* she persuaded my grandmother to pay for a rented house in London for each summer season, supposedly for my benefit; I would not have minded it for a month, but we went to London at the beginning of May and stayed till the end of July. For most of the time I was bored rigid.

In the late summer of 1935 Frances Cole and I had gone on a voyage on a windjammer from Belfast to Abo, in Finland, the last leg of the ship's homeward voyage from Australia in ballast. The next summer Uncle Egghead offered to take Frances and me with him to New Zealand, where he was going for a fishing expedition. We would, he warned us, be on our own when we got to New Zealand. I was forbidden to go. It appeared that the White Slave Traffic was even more rampant in New Zealand than in the whole of Europe. Henry broke in on this interdiction to say: "If you don't let Ursula go, you'll look a fool. Abo is the depot of the White Slave Trade in Europe, and you had no objection to her going there."

When we were alone together, I said to Henry, goggle-eyed: "Is that really true?"

"Goodness knows," he told me, "but it did as an argument."

My grandmother, who was nobody's fool, probably realised that what my mother was frightened of was the loss of the excuse for the rented house in London. She very sweetly announced that she would pay the expenses of the trip, because "travel opens the windows of the mind." It was a shrewd crack at my mother, who had no interest in abroad and distrusted all foreigners below the rank of ambassador.

Egghead, Frances and I duly set off from Tilbury Docks on 13 March 1935, on the cargo ship, *Port Hobart*, which carried twelve passengers. The passengers were on the dull side. Two young midshipmen were pleasant company and we played Cribbage with them in the evenings.

I shall always be grateful to the 3rd Officer who insisted that I left my bunk at crack of dawn during our passage through the Panama Canal, to see the movingly evocative memorial stone let into the canal bank in memory of all those who had died during its construction.

There were two stops of several days at Kingston, Jamaica and Suva, Fiji. We took the opportunity to explore both islands. Otherwise, the monotony ate into my soul.

We were not due to land at Christchurch, New Zealand, until 28 April. When we came out into the Pacific Ocean I went, accompanied by Frances, to the galley and begged the cook for work. He was an efficient young Tynesider. Not by the blink of an eyelid did he betray any surprise at such a request from a couple of passengers. He set us up, on the deck outside the galley, with a mountain of potatoes to peel. From then on we reported for work every morning and peeled potatoes for the entire ship's company. It was in no way boring: the crew members paused in their duties for a chat and were far better company than the passengers. I tried to ginger up the cook to introduce some variety into the rather monotonous fare served at the captain's table. In this I failed. You cannot alter a code of practice in any of the Services.

The other passengers looked askance at what they considered lack of good breeding and levity of conduct, but the 'Old Man', Captain Kippings, gave the project his full blessing. He was a delightful, genial officer. He and Egghead, who had served in the Navy, exchanged many nautical yarns.

The only time I felt that Captain Kippings overreacted was on an occasion when, nearing New Zealand I thought it of passing interest to announce, at the breakfast table, that my toenails had unaccountably all fallen off during the night. Egghead was thunderstruck and the Captain smote his brow and cried: "My God, this *would* happen after we dropped the doctor at Suva!"

I was profoundly shocked. My biographical reading had made me aware that Henry VIII had suffered precisely the same symptoms, and that they had been ascribed to syphilis. What I had not expected was that it should be instantly taken for granted that I had brought the contagion aboard.

When we were established at a respectable guest house at Christchurch and Egghead had departed on his fishing trip, our thoughts reverted to our friends on the *Port Hobart*, which was tied up at the port of Lyttelton, divided from Christchurch by a range of not inconsiderable hills. We spent one day scaling these peaks and slithering down the far side; quite a feat. When we turned up, breathless, at the gangplank, it was to be greeted with more astonishment than enthusiasm.

For the homeward journey we embarked at Wellington on the Shaw Savill liner *Wairangi*. Here there was a strict segregation line between passengers and crew. Thankfully the journey took exactly one month, from June 13 to July 13, instead of nearly two. We made one brief stop at Las Palmas and had the misfortune to round the Horn at night. I did rise and peer over the port rail at an ill-defined land mass.

I think I must be a reincarnated emigrant of early times, since the restrictions of a ship have, for me, a prison atmosphere, made worse by the air of false jollity that invariably prevails. Better, really, to be battened down. That, at least, would dispose of the jollity.

On our return to England, my mother staged a dramatic refutation of whatever suspicions her initial decision not to let me go on the trip had excited. I arrived at my grandmother's house just before luncheon. I remember my mother hurtling down the stairs to where I stood in the hall, surrounded by my luggage, and clasping me to her bosom, — a thing she had never done before, nor yet was ever to do again — declaring that it was so wonderful to have me safely home that she was going to cancel her luncheon date in order to enjoy every moment of my reappearance in the family circle. This is the only instance I remember of my mother mistiming her entrance and hamming her clearly perceived role. Her daughter's genuine act of total bewilderment seems, in hindsight, to have decided her that we should not, in future, appear on her personal stage together.

My grandmother's maxim that one should travel in order to open the windows of one's mind was excellent advice, which I was more than ready to take. Brenda, also, was keen to extend the boundaries of her environment. The following spring we found ourselves a tour by which, for the outlay of £36, we could board a Yugoslavian steamer at Trieste, voyage down the Adriatic coast, calling in at all the ports of interest and proceed, via Corfu, to Piraeus, the port of Athens. After a stop of four days, an Italian ship would convey us to Bari, on the east coast of Italy. In Italy we would travel by train, first to Naples, to explore Pompeii and Herculaneum, and finally entrain for home, via Rome and Paris.

Although particularly open-minded by nature and intention, the distressing and repressive arguments that preceded the New Zealand venture drove me to subterfuge on this occasion. Fearful of invoking the frenzy of the previous year, I arranged with Brenda to meet me in Florence, where I had parental permission to be.

My uncle, Hugh Wyndham, and his wife Maud, née Lyttelton, (I had two Aunt Mauds) were accustomed to rent, for the month of May, a villa in the grounds of a castello called Poggio Gherardo, situated in the hills behind Fiesole, from which one had a view of Florence, spread out in the plain below. I was happy and lucky to be their annual guest. Aunt Maud had a deep knowledge of the arts and was an inspirational guide to Florence and Venice. Brenda was a great favourite of theirs and they readily agreed to let her stay a night before our departure to Trieste.

While staying with my uncle and aunt it was my habit, on afternoons when there was nothing else planned, to take an orange from the bowl in the dining room and roam the hillside in the sunshine, eating my orange at the moment that I turned my steps towards home. I very seldom met another human being. Occasionally a peasant was on the same path as myself. He civilly stepped to one side, we exchanged *buon giornos,* and went our separate ways. I was frankly incredulous and derisive when Uncle Hugh told me that his landlord, Mr Gordon Waterfield of Poggio Gherardo, had chided my uncle for allowing me to walk unattended in what, it appeared, was lustful territory.

My mother made an extraordinary fuss if I went for a walk before breakfast at home in Leicestershire, refusing to accept that any sane person would do so eccentric a thing and demanding, menacingly, what I had been doing? When I asked what she supposed I had been up to, she looked embarrassed as well as cross and demanded again that I should name an activity other than walking.

Now this nonsense had followed me to Italy. Uncle Hugh naturally felt that Mr Waterfield must know more of the implicit dangers than a visitor like himself could, and also felt some responsibility for his niece's virtue and well-being. He insisted on accompanying me. I think a brigand could easily have overpowered Uncle Hugh; but we enjoyed our walks together.

I wrote to my mother, informing her, with becoming innocent excitement, of the purportedly sudden inspiration of a plan for the Yugoslav tour, so that she would only get the letter after our departure from Florence.

The year before, Edward VIII and Mrs Simpson had made roughly the same tour on the yacht *Nahlin*. A French-speaking Yugoslav in Split had seen the couple and had not been impressed. When we canvassed his opinion he shrugged his shoulders and could think of no more to say than that Mrs Simpson was very old. In this context an old American woman from Cincinnatti, who was a fellow-voyager, thought differently. I quote from an account that I wrote at the time.

> She had travelled all over the world and always alone. As far as we could gather, Russia was the only country she had not been to. She was an ex-school mistress, so how she found the money to travel so incessantly I cannot imagine. She was now on her way to India, via Beirut and some desert. I admired her courage tremendously. She was fun and a great character and we were awfully nice to her throughout the voyage, which I think gave her pleasure; but we spoilt it all at the end by going off and forgetting to say goodbye.
>
> There was one thing about her that annoyed me, and that was her implicit belief that the relationship between the Duke of Windsor and Mrs Simpson was one of the most beautiful, inspiring and uplifting romances that the world has ever known. Her sentimentality on the subject nearly drove me mad, the more so that her conviction was so strong that it would have been useless and unpleasant to have argued with her.

I have already remarked that social conditions in Northern Ireland were at least fifty years behind the mainland. I quote once more, with reference to Frances Cole of Florence Court:

I taught Brenda a bad habit on this voyage: that of bell-ringing.
I had only lately learned it myself, from Frances, on our way to
New Zealand. Before that I had been accustomed to wearing my
legs out, running all over the ship, in often useless search,
whenever I wanted a steward. I was complaining to Frances
about not being able to find him one evening. She said casually:
'Why not ring the bell?' I was shocked by such grand ideas and
expostulated, but Frances explained to me that presumably the
bell had been put there to be rung, therefore why not ring it?
Despite myself, I was impressed by this sound argument. I rang
it, rather half-heartedly. It was answered at once, which so
surprised and enchanted me that I became an inveterate
bellringer from that moment.

I suggested to Brenda that she should ring our cabin bell one
evening, when she wanted her hot water bottle or something or
other, just before going to bed. I was amused that she was just as
horrified and used the same arguments against it as I had to
Frances. In reply I brought out the old gag about the bell being
there to be rung, and added a new one, to the effect that the
stewards were paid to answer it; money always being a good line
of argument with B. She said, doubtfully, that she thought it
would do no harm to ring it this once, and did so. Thus the habit
began.

The steward who knew English was attached to the dining
room and really had nothing to do with the cabins at all, but the
poor man always had to answer our bell, as he was the only one
who understood what we wanted. He was very patient and nice
about it and I don't think minded, because he wished us a happy
journey when we left, which cheered us a good deal.

While at home, one rang the bell whenever one wanted the fire
making up, the curtains drawn or the waste paper basket emptied,
in a manner that now strikes me as absurd, since it would have
been simpler to have performed these tasks oneself, but those who
did them were engaged and paid for the purpose. No such service
was expected outside the home. In Ulster, in the left-over time
warp from the Edwardian period, Ann and Frances Cole had their
clothes pulled onto them and were buttoned into them by their
maid, as if they were still wearing tight-laced corsets and dresses

with bodices with hooks all down the back.

Back on board the *Beograd* the passenger list changed, to some extent, at every port of call. Some passengers left the ship and others embarked in their place. Those allotted to our table in the dining saloon were always English speakers. We started off with an Italian, whose immaculate English he claimed to have perfected at Cambridge University. He was pleasant company, but he had a disturbing bee in his bonnet: Culture. He spoke of little else. This upset Brenda: "What can he think of us?" she wailed. But I don't know that, for myself, I greatly cared. The talk at dinner turned on the English royal family. The Italian dismissed them as useless, in a sentence: they were, he said, lacking in culture.

We were unable to visit the island of Corfu, since only passengers who did not intend to return to the *Beograd* were allowed to disembark there. We finally left the steamer at Piraeus. It was a tedious entry, involving standing in two queues, one to inform a Greek official of our ancestry back to the third generation; the second to reveal how much money we were carrying. My truthful declaration that I had no more than the equivalent of nine English pounds, met with disbelief, leaving me with the fear that I did, indeed, lack the financial means of ever returning to England. On leaving the last of these travelling hazards we fell prey to a Greek con-man called Thomas Danabassis, the second of a heartless band of people who rooked us with perfect ease.

T. Danabassis was a grubby moth-eaten little man with 'Official Interpreter' written on a band round his arm. He asked us which hotel we were going to and, on hearing its name, announced that he came from there. Before we realized what was happening, he had bundled us into a taxi, flung our luggage in on top of us and driven away with us, who knew where. He did point out the sights as we drove along and, on his indicating the Parthenon, it came back to me that the Acropolis was not, after all, a temple, but a hill with temples on top. Brenda, too, confessed that she had hitherto been uncertain of the relative situations of the Parthenon and the Acropolis.

On booking in at the hotel, Thomas Danabassis handed me a sheet of paper with a lot of squiggles on it and the sum 136 drachmas written plainly underneath. "What", I asked, "is this? The taxi cannot possibly have cost as much." T. Danabassis explained that the residue was in the nature of a reward for his having, willy nilly, pushed us into the taxi and occupying a seat that might otherwise have held the luggage that we had been forced to bear the full weight of ourselves. I was weak in the face of the self-confident stare in Thomas Danabassis's beady eyes and told him coldly to collect the money from the man at the desk. Seeing that I was displeased, Thomas Danabassis delivered the Parthian shot of claiming that he had fought for my country in the late war: therefore it was now up to me to do something for him in exchange.

When we went to Cook's Athens office to claim our reservations on the Italian liner, *Campidoglio,* sailing for Naples in four days time, it was to be told that the ship was already fully booked and that our reservation, made in Florence, had not been received. Tired of being submissive, we became rather high-handed in tone. Especially on receiving the information that the next ship did not leave till a fortnight later. We told them haughtily that we had neither the money nor the inclination to stay in Athens for a fortnight; and, that as they had got us into this predicament, it was up to them to get us out. We thereby learnt the lesson that it is imprudent to be less than civil to those in control.

We were told, that there was a very nice Greek steamer, called the *Thraki,* leaving for Brindisi in three days time. From there we could go overland, by train, to Naples. The *Thraki* turned out to be a dirty old hulk which had, in common with the Red Lion at Dolgelly, the disadvantage that there was nothing to put in your belly and no one to answer the bell. What food there was was revolting, but we told each other, philosophically, that we could easily exist on bread and cheese for three days. However, the cheese, when it appeared, was pale green. We felt that there was a limit to the number of risks we should take. We existed on a diet of oranges and chocolate biscuits that we had brought aboard with us. The captain, a man of equally unappetising appearance, smelt so strongly of violets that one became aware of his approach some time before his presence.

Our cabin was so small that we could not both stand up in it at the same time. The bunks, at right angles to each other, were so short that our toes, perforce, became inter-plaited during the night. There was no hope of washing ourselves. This was made less of a privation by our recollections of having a bath aboard the *Beograd*. It had been necessary to give the order an hour in advance and most of the crew had been mustered to the task. When we finally descended to the scene of action it had been necessary to grope our way through overwhelming clouds of steam, guided to the bathroom by the weird and soul-shattering groaning of the water pipes. Men were dashing in and out, regulating things. When we had finally cleared the last assistant out, and got in, some terrible complication had invariably arisen: such as the hot water tap stuck in the on position, or the plug came out all by itself and disappeared, or there was a minor explosion somewhere. In such a situation, we screamed for help and huddled, pressing towels against our nakedness, while the whole company surged in again and righted the difficulty.

After the ruthless exploitation from the Greeks, the kindly Italian spirit soon had us in thrall. The train stopped at Bari and an official-sounding voice on the platform announced, in English, "the train stops here for forty-five minutes." Having remarked what very lengthy stops Italian trains did make at some stations, we had no difficulty in believing this information. Descending leisurely, we went off to buy some food: two cartons of macaroni, two ham rolls, some cherries and a bottle of water each. Heavily weighed down, we strolled along the platform as in a dream. Suddenly we heard a terrific uproar and raised our eyes to see the train slowly steaming out of the station. The porters were rushing up and down gesticulating and uttering hoarse cries to attract our attention. We fairly hurtled across the platform and many willing hands heaved us into the last coach of all. Coming from a country where it was a crime to enter a moving train and the porters had no eyes for any but those who had engaged them to carry baggage and from whom they could expect a tip, we were much impressed by and grateful to the public-spirited porters of Bari.

Arriving in Naples, we booked into a hotel overlooking the

Bay and noted that the Italian Fleet was in port. The next day was spent exploring Pompeii and Herculaneum and evading the determined advances of the Italian version of Thomas Dababassis. He had already trapped four foolish English, including the perennial tourist, hung with cameras. One of his victims, pointing to the words, 'Viva il Duce' scrawled on a wall, said: "I keep on seeing that everywhere. What does it mean?" Brenda told her that it was the Italian for a Merry Christmas. I have no reason to suppose that she was not believed. Back in Naples, the night before our departure we walked round the bay after dinner. After a time we noticed that two Naval officers were keeping in step with us a few paces behind. We discussed, in piercing voices, the possibility that we were being followed; oblivious of the possibility that the men might understand English. We doubled back on our tracks and so did they. We stopped at a postcard kiosk, and they silently stood close behind us, hemming us in. We turned and broke hastily through their ranks, at which one, a smart looking officer of very pleasing appearance and mien, came alongside us, saluted smartly and said to me, who was walking on the outside: "We speak English. May we come with you and talk to you?" I turned to Brenda for the confirmation that I felt sure that I would get from her to this pleasant proposal. Surprisingly, she was walking along with her eyes turned devoutly to the ground, like a demure nun. She appeared lost in meditation. Shy as I was, I felt unequal to coping with two Italian Naval officers while hampered by the presence of a demure nun. Embarrassed, I turned towards the young man and murmured: "I don't think you'd better." He saluted again, said: "I am sorry", and disappeared out of our lives forever. I felt that I had handled the situation clumsily and Brenda was more than ready to agree with me.

The next morning we rose at 5 am to catch the train to Rome and Paris and, thence, home. We had expected to pass straight through Rome, but it appeared that we were travelling with special cheap tickets for the purpose of visiting an exhibition, the nature of which had not been made known to us. It was necessary to get them stamped at the exhibition entrance. In those days of primitive travel, Thomas Cook filled a need now totally neglected, by having representatives at railway stations who were happy to perform any menial service to make the traveller's lot easy. We despatched one of these excellent men to get the tickets stamped and directed our own steps towards St Peter's. As we ascended the steps, a stranger rushed after us in an agitated manner to explain unnecessarily that we could not enter the sacred portals with bare arms. As I was carrying a coat and Brenda a rug in which to envelop ourselves, we were startled by this unlooked for approach, supposing that somebody had pinned rude notices secretly on our backs, or that our dresses were falling off; even possibly, in this hitherto unknown country, that we had broken some archaic law and that the police were after us. We gave the interfering stranger short shrift. For what purpose did he suppose that we had burdened ourselves with coat and rug?

On the train to Paris we fell in with the Italian army. We would be sleeping on the train and hoped to secure a compartment to ourselves. We found such a compartment and spread our belongings over every seat. A man in military uniform came to the door and, surveying the loaded seats, enquired interrogatively: "Occupato?" "Si," we said sternly, "occupato." All seemed well until, just before the train started, the man returned, with two comrades, and they calmly moved our luggage on to the racks and sat down. We were playing a card game called Spider. The man seated by Brenda pointed at the cards and said "Pok*air*?" I did not understand what he meant, but Brenda explained brightly that no it was not Poker, but Spider. They thought this the most extraordinary word and practised saying it without much success. They spoke no English, nor really any French, but the one called Xavier, who was sitting by me, could write a few words of English, though he had no notion how to pronounce them. Alberto, who was quiet and self-effacing behind his spectacles, understood a little French, which was helpful. Xavier and Lamberto, who was sitting beside Brenda and had made the Poker observation, had strong personalities and dominated the scene. Alberto scarcely got a look in, except once, when they pulled him forward as an exhibit, to claim that his was a *nomme Inglese*. Occasionally, when they could not grasp our sign language, they called upon Alberto in the hope that he would understand our French. They asked what we did at home in England. This was awkward. It sounded too feeble to indicate: nothing. After due consultation we waved our hands about in an instinctive effort to make things clear, and murmured, "la chasse". They appeared much interested and went through the motions of firing a gun. Disabused of that idea, they bumped up and down in their seats, as one who rides a horse. Great was their sense of achievement when this hypothesis proved correct. I added the word *'volpe'* as further information and, to my surprise, was understood. Another chastener was that they then wanted to know what our fathers did. Two army colonels sounded, and was received as, dull. Why did we not make up a more interesting background? They wanted to know where, in England, the Emperor of Ethiopia had taken refuge, but had never heard of the city of Bath, so, after many gesticulations, we settled for purveying the false information that the ex-Emperor and suite dwelt in London.

Lamberto, who was very good looking, and knew it, asked Brenda to marry him. She made signs that she had no wish to marry immediately. He then asked me. I reflected on the various possibilities of the result of saying yes, but made it known that I wished to marry an Englishman, which was considered deplorably insular. Lamberto, now at the top of his form, seized a piece of paper and wrote on it 'Henrico VIII'. He then went through the motions of cutting off our heads. As the train drew near the station where they were to get out, Xavier snatched Lamberto's paper and pencil and wrote upon it: 'You are ill that you cannot come with us.' Lamberto took a ring from my finger, put it on one of Brenda's, linked his arm with hers and announced: "Mistress". Xavier, with great enjoyment, found the confidence to say the words: "No, bad, bad." When they left the train, they came and stood on the platform, by our window. Lamberto gave a moving performance of sobbing into his handkerchief. Before the train stopped they had suggested that we get off with them. They would like, they said, to take us batheing and we could then continue our journey on a later train. As we watched them drive away in a horse-drawn van, with many comrades, we wondered whether we, too, would have been sandwiched into the van with the troops if we had accepted their invitation.

With their departure the pleasing notion returned of having the compartment to ourselves. This was shattered at Pisa, as night began to fall, by the unwanted entrance of an elderly man, followed, all too soon, by a crowd of professional cyclists, making for Paris and a *tour de France*. They spent the entire night prowling about the train, entering the compartment, sitting down, getting up and recycling the prowling process. The old man added to our exasperation by repeating, at intervals, what splendid young fellows they were. By the time we reached Paris we had learnt, the hard way, that passive resistance is what the authorities find it hardest to cope with. We established ourselves, in all innocence, on the platform, before the train came in. It appeared that this was a heinous crime. Every available official was called upon to remove us. We sat tight and told them amiably that we were doing no harm. They finally retired, in high dudgeon and desperately wounded pride. The only person who really enjoyed the encounter was our porter, who thought the whole episode highly amusing.

We crossed the Channel in a thunderstorm and did not reach London until nearly midnight — half an hour late. Such unpunctuality was, at that time, unusual. I was thankful to find that my parents' car and chauffeur had come to Victoria Station to meet us. I had returned with not one penny in my purse. The date was June 9th 1937.

I had returned to England distinctly nervous of being severely castigated by my mother for wandering about Europe without her permission. To my surprise, no condemnation was uttered. It was not until sometime later that I discovered that she had used more subtle means to give expression to her disapprobation. She told Aunt Maud that Brenda was not a fit travelling companion, on account of her sexual immorality. She did not bother to check with me that Brenda's conduct abroad was, surprisingly, in complete contrast to her behaviour at home. My mother knew that this information would distress my uncle and aunt. I was admiringly grateful to them in that, with a charity that I failed to find at home, they continued to show great kindness to Brenda.

FATHERS AND DAUGHTERS

*T*HE SAME age as myself, Brenda was called 'Pug' by her adoring father, because of the shape of her nose. She had enormous zest for life and, before the problems that she brought upon herself, accumulated with the passing of the years a genuine and kindly interest in people. She would draw out those labelled by others dull, stodgy, uninteresting, so that they sparkled and showed themselves in a light hitherto unsuspected. She was passionate, hot-tempered, but also quick to see the funny side or find a way round an awkward situation. A non-smoker, when somebody gave her a cigarette lighter, she was entranced and thought only of how to turn it to good account.

"Look at it," she said to me. "Isn't it neat? You know, one could crouch over it on winter evenings."

Those who knew of her promiscuity found our friendship a matter for mirth: the chaste and the unchaste. Between 1933 and 1936 Brenda had two abortions. At that time the operation was illegal in this country. For the first she journeyed to Paris and something rather horrendous took place on a kitchen table. The necessity for the second she confessed to her parents. Whether she felt unable to face the events in Paris a second time, or had been unable to get funds for the second operation, I do not know. The removal of the foetus was performed in London, by a doctor who must have been heavily bribed. The day after, I visited Brenda, reclining in a bed, at the Langham Hotel. She looked ghastly and completely bloodless. It was this second operation that I suffered for in a vicarious fashion.

Mrs Alexander, in her acute anxiety concerning every aspect of the disastrous situation in which her daughter had involved her, confessed its cause to a neighbour, who just happened to be one of my mother's Bridge-playing cronies. If tea goes with sympathy, Bridge goes with scandal. My mother had never sat on a secret in her life. It took me years to become aware that her crushing retort to a plea not to pass on a confidence — "I don't know anybody who would be interested" — in her view absolved her from any understood promise. She made a highly dramatic story of it to my father. I would have thought that the foreseen result would have bored her as much as it disturbed and irritated me, in about equal quantities. Dinner time became a nightmare. Evening after evening the repetition ground on about the disgrace, the evil intention, the unclean life, varied only by what *I* might expect if I got into a similar predicament. I was to understand, he reiterated, that I would have to keep the baby. He would see to that. The event appeared to have been foreseen, prepared for and a code of practice laid down. I was not expected to speak and did not. But I was puzzled. In my innocent and ignorant mind it was irreconcilable that my father, who, following his creed that the truth was the most important basic fact in the conduct of life, had made clear that he considered me ill-favoured and stupid, and my mother, who stated that no man who came to our house was a friend of mine, could yet suppose that the sight of me would arouse uncontrollable passion in a male. This simplistic theory led to me having to overcome an irrational sexual fear when I was at length free to make my own decisions and find answers to all these unvoiced questions. I do, however, date from this episode the period when I first began to doubt the omniscience of this alarming parent.

Brenda's relationship with her father was the exact opposite of mine. Colonel Alexander, a delightful, understanding, unjudging man, sustained by a deep, unspoken religious faith, adored his elder daughter. Later on he was to remark to me: "With all Pug's faults, one cannot help loving her." I agreed wholeheartedly. Had he used the word "trust", I would have been obliged to disassociate myself from his views.

After bolting from two successive husbands, Brenda proposed to throw in her lot in Dublin with a married, Roman Catholic, Irish adventurer. Her father exacted from her a promise that she would reconsider this decision. Brenda gave him her solemn vow — and left for Ireland the same week. To me she said that she did mean to think her future over very seriously, but that alone in the west of Ireland seemed to her the best, in fact the *only* place, where a sensible decision could be made. I did not reply. I think we understood each other.

Her defection to Dublin, broke her father's heart. It may be safe to put one's faith in one's God, but it is a measure of the lack of understanding between fathers and daughters at that and in earlier times, that even Colonel Alexander should have been so unaware of his daughter's uncontrollable emotions, that led her to make any declaration that would momentarily take the pressure off a fraught situation.

My own father was a man of rigid puritan principles. Adultery was quite the worst sin listed in the Commandments. He had a hero worship for General Eisenhower during the War, until my brother John told him that the General was carrying on with his A.T.S. driver. I well remember the stricken look on my father's face. He longed not to believe it, but my brother was in a position to know, and he trusted his word. Eisenhower's name never crossed my father's lips from that moment.

His lack of trust in his daughter went to astonishing lengths. When War broke out we were holidaying in a rented cottage in Sussex. I was summoned to London to join my Red Cross unit. On my first weekend leave I telephoned my parents to suggest spending it with them. (War had a very unifying effect on everybody.) The offer was at first accepted, but later my mother telephoned to say that John had got in touch, with a similar proposal. Of course, his was the first priority and I must now make other arrangements. I pointed out that the one spare room contained two beds and John would presumably not be occupying both of them.

"I thought of that," explained my mother, "but your father won't hear of it."

Later, my mother, who in every area that did not interfere with her personal pleasures, had a strong family feeling, rang back to say that she had sent her maid away on a holiday for which she was due. I could occupy the maid's bedroom.

My natural fear of my father was overcome by resentment of his extraordinary suspicions. On my arrival, I confronted him: "Do you honestly suppose that I would commit incest with John?"

My father was reading a book. He did not bother to lower it. From behind its pages he intoned: "I really don't know, but there is a lot of it about in the slums."

The General Strike of 1926 had granted the childish desires of many gentlemen of leisure, who rushed off to become engine drivers or the like. Of the privations and poverty that caused the strike, I heard no mention. By the early 1930s I was old enough to feel that I ought to know something of what was going on beyond my own narrow world, but had to admit that reading the newspapers bored me beyond endurance. Boredom had become my bugbear during adolescence. I persevered however and, from this source, learnt of a project that Peter Scott was organising to create work for at least a number of the great mass of unemployed. I wish that I could remember details of this admirable endeavour. Funds were asked for and, having always equated myself with the underdog, I sent a mite.

My father's one charitable work was as chairman of the Waifs and Strays Society, now renamed, in the present frenzy to avoid admitting that anybody has problems, The Children's Society. I still think that the words "waif" and "stray" grip the heart and engender, in their very sound, an instant desire to help. My father played up this line for all it was worth. He became a totally different personality in the course of the speeches he composed and orated to get funds for this charity. Expressions like "poor little mites", "helpless kiddies", "tiny orphans", a jargon that we were forbidden to use at home, flowed from his lips in a voice breaking with emotion. Afterwards, when we expressed our disgust he agreed that it was not a mode of speech that he would permit off a public platform, but that he found it made people open their purses a great deal more readily than higher rhetoric. It was a side of him only genuine waifs and strays ever got to know.

My mother, for a few years, filled the post of County Commissioner of the Girl Guides. Unlike my father, she brought no enthusiasm to her role and wore her uniform, although faultlessly tailored, rather as though it had broad arrows on it.

By contrast, the dedication that my father put into his work for the Waifs and Strays continues to astonish me. He did not only raise funds for them; he visited the Homes, where he actually beheld the waifs, who were, of course, no longer straying. Could that have been the motive — his rigid puritanical prejudice?

To this day I instinctively regard Adultery as the Cardinal Sin. What is, in fact, meant by sinning.

Some years ago I read in a Sunday newspaper that it was taking a census on the experience of being a long-term mistress, and invited telephone calls. My keen curiosity, not any wish to bare my love life, led me to dial the number. A young male voice with an American accent answered.

"What," I asked, "is an American doing, conducting this sort of investigation for an English paper?"

"I am not an American," the voice told me, "I come from Belfast. I am an out-of-work actor. Actors can assume any accent. I decided that an American accent would get me further than an Irish one."

He then proceeded to ask me a string of not well thought out questions. When he came to "What did you find most enjoyable about the relationship?", my father's daughter replied: "I don't think mere enjoyment, as such, is precisely relevant to a long-term relationship. I spent the first years feeling guilty about committing adultery and then was shocked when I reached the point of no longer feeling a sense of guilt."

The American accent fell away and it was the Ulsterman who replied: "Ah, I know, it was the same with myself."

It remains a surprise to me that my father's puritanical sense of moral rectitude did not include any burst of rhetoric against homosexuals. He was twelve years old when Lord Queensberry, in the law case he brought against Oscar Wilde, let his son, and the whole side, down. One views now, with a sense of astonishment, how Victorian fathers engaged homosexuals, like Oscar Browning, to instil in their young sons a sense of physical purity. This surreal fantasy would appear to have loomed large in many papas of the period.

It had not always been so. At the age of nineteen, Lord Byron wrote, from Cambridge, to a provincial Miss Pigott, a neighbour of his mother at Southwell, in Nottinghamshire, to inform her that he had fallen desperately in love with a choirboy of King's College Chapel. I doubt if even the most sophisticated young women of the 20th century have often been the recipients of such a confession from a youth still testing his ultimate sexual affiliations. Miss Pigott, aged twenty-two, must have sent a sympathetic answer, for another letter from Lord Byron on the same subject was despatched to her. I would like to know more about this compassionate girl, but the Pigotts no longer live at Southwell.

As regards Byron and the choirboy, the love proved lasting, possibly helped by absence and the recognition of another soul in torment. When three years later, in 1809, Byron, then abroad, heard of the young man's death due to the misuse of drugs, he sent a howl of bereavement to his friend, John Cam Hobhouse, in England, describing the dead man as the only person whom he had ever truly loved.

Natural bisexuality in men is rare, if indeed it exists. Ultimate sexual attraction, when unmotivated by other considerations, comes down in lasting favour of one sex. Byron's indiscriminate sexual history would seem to bespeak a narcissism that found, in any admiration, a reassuring indication of the reality behind the reflection.

It is widely assumed that the last straw that broke Lady Byron's marital back was her husband's desire to bugger her. Lady Melbourne, the aunt who had got her into the marriage that ruined her peace of mind for all time, could have told her that this is, unfortunately, a not uncommon proposal among husbands and lovers. Her aunt probably did so inform her, when it was too late.

Throughout the 18th and 19th centuries many younger sons did not marry, and lived out their lives behind the park wall owned by their father, then their brother and, possibly, eventually, their nephew. If their valet did more for them than keep their clothes in good order, nobody saw fit to comment on it.

In the 1930s impoverished young men, earning a living in London, often shared lodgings to lighten expenses. This necessity put a question mark on their relationships which, among the couples I knew, turned out to be wholly heterosexual. After seeing a play, in which the lead part was magnificently acted by a widely respected actor, I was foolish enough to enthuse to my mother that I thought he was wonderful. The only reply that I got was an abrupt and explicit "I don't like pansies". It was like a slap in the face to a young girl. I had not been aware of the man's sexual preferences, and they had nothing to do with his status as an actor or as an attractive man seen on stage.

A startling exception to this dislike of "pansies" was the beautiful and decadent Stephen Tennant. He was related to my father, but I do not think that would have been sufficient to save him, had not my mother greatly enjoyed the friendship of his beautiful, witty and bitchy sister, Clare.[1] She remains the most beautiful woman I remember seeing; surpassing Lady Diana Cooper, in that Clare's face was not a beautiful mask, but enhanced by an ever varying play of expression. She was always very nice to me. I have noticed, with some surprise, that beautiful, worldly women often take the trouble to be kind to shy, nervous girls, whom one would expect them to completely overlook. She kept most of her bitchiness for her three husbands, whom she thought perfect until she was married to them, when she quickly tired of their society and lost no opportunity to let them know, in language carefully chosen to wound, just how stupid she thought they were.

When Stephen Tennant died, it was revealed to the public that

---

[1] Both children of the youngest of "The Three Graces".

121

he was the individual on whom the character of Sebastian Flyte in *Brideshead Revisited* is based. It will be remembered that Sebastian's inseparable companion was a teddy bear. In the case of Stephen Tennant his *alter ego* was a tortoise. All the light went out of his life when the tortoise fell gravely ill. Its life was despaired of. However, the crisis came and went, the tortoise survived and, after an anxious convalescence, was restored to full animation and health. But how, my mother had enquired, in uncomprehending amazement, can you cure a sick tortoise? Stephen's reply was reassuring in its simplicity. "Just by loving it," he told her. The notion of loving a tortoise unlocked some closed door in my mother's heart and she told and retold the story with a depth of emotion I had not realised that she had in her.

After World War II, my mother, in the changing climate of opinion, found it suitable, and enlivening to the conversation round her lunch table, to invite to her house Bobby Shaw, the son of Nancy Astor by her first marriage, and another man, whose mother was a friend of hers. The second choice was later dropped when he imprudently got into trouble with the police, due to what a mutual acquaintance described as his 'al fresco habits'. Bobby Shaw was a most amusing, though deeply unhappy, man. He had been offered the chance to clear out of the country in the '20s, but had courageously preferred to stay and go to prison. He had to resign his commission in the Household Cavalry and his greatest friend and brother officer, Hugh, last Earl of Sefton, of Croxteth Hall, Liverpool, never spoke to him again. (If you can call that the behaviour of a great friend.)

Lord Sefton was, I think, the handsomest man I have ever seen, since he combined classically regular features with a tremendous sense of personal style and a natural air of high breeding. Style, as personified then by Noel Coward and Gertrude Lawrence — a subtle blend of carriage, bearing, grace and ease of manner — is virtually dead now, on stage and off. To see the amiable Julie Andrews endeavouring to reproduce any sense⁻ of Gertrude Lawrence, was to make one weep. When I occasionally find an individual who displays a vestige of this lost art, a sense of elation animates me. Michael Parkinson is a solitary case in point. He does not need to play to the gallery, in contrast to his successors on television.

Lord Sefton had a bachelor uncle, Major Dick Molyneux, known to the wits of Society as 'The Penny Steamer', because he stopped at every peer. I wonder if the nephew had been covering up for his uncle and the strain of shouldering another such secret was too much for him? I do not know.

I recall a family dinner party at which Bobby Shaw was present, soon after Lord Astor died. Bobby was grieved at not having featured in his step-father's will. A cousin said consolingly: "It was only because Uncle Waldorf knew you were well provided for. You know he loved you, Bobby."

"Love!" proclaimed Mr Shaw, with huge contempt. "What good is that to me? I can get love for thirty shillings whenever I want it."

I mentally registered that it came much more expensive for heterosexuals.

Bobby Shaw had a dramatic end of his own timing and devising. It became his habit to take an overdose and then ring up all his friends and relations to say goodbye. Of course they rushed round in a body and rescued him. The compulsion to say goodbye must have been irresistible since, in order to carry out his purpose successfully, Bobby paid an American Air Force pilot £400 for his suicide pill. But still the goodbye calls were made. This time, though, the family and friends arrived too late. There was one other difference from the usual routine. Bobby telephoned and took the pill from his lover's flat, during the man's absence. Thus it was Bobby's friend's front door that was battered down by the fire brigade, not Bobby's.

To return for a last look at Lord Sefton. He had been turned down, when a young man, by Edwina Ashley in favour of Lord Louis Mountbatten. He then let it be understood that he would never marry because there was a taint of madness in his family. In 1941, at the age of forty-three, he married one of the Mrs Simpson set, an American divorcee called Mrs Josephine Gwynne, but known as Foxy to her friends. During their marriage Lady Sefton discovered that her husband, in a very old-fashioned manner, was maintaining a mistress in Brighton. She told him that all she wanted in life was his happiness, so that, if he wanted to make his mistress his wife, he had only to say so and Lady Sefton would agree to a divorce. Such altruism surely called for a warmer response than a laconic: "Aw Foxy, don't talk balls!"

As usual in those circumstances, no more was said on the subject.

WAR
CORRESPONDENCE

*I*N THE SUMMER of 1939 when the imminent declaration of war was clearly inevitable, I had joined the V.A.D because I thought women looked stupid strutting about in uniform and drilling on a barrack square. It took only the week's intensive training at Lambeth hospital, on a different ward each day, to bring home to me the depressing fact that I only liked people as individuals, not *en masse*. I did not want to touch the patients, and the diseases from which they were suffering as often as not repulsed me, instead of arousing sympathy and a sense of care. The cancer ward was the most harrowing. None of the patients had had the nature of their complaint named to them. One woman said to me: "Isn't it wonderful, nurse. I've begun menstruating again; and me sixty-two!". I was told to feed spoonfuls of stodgy hospital food to a young girl who was in the mortuary before I left the ward that evening.

A very pretty, flirtatious girl got round a doctor to let her into the operating theatre to watch a caesarian section. I was deeply envious of this initiative and full of questions concerning the experience. All she could think of to relate was that the amount of blood about had been unbelievable.

We were given instruction on the anatomy by a nurse who led us up to the plaster cast of a human torso. She removed the top half to reveal all the organs hung on hooks within the framework, so that they could be removed and examined. There appeared, to me, to be one important omission.

"I say," I asked eagerly, "where is the womb?"

"That's enough of that, nurse," snapped the instructress, and replaced the front of the torso.

While my colleague was watching the buckets-of-blood operation, I had been handed a pair of tweezers and told to delouse — or was it de-nit? — a patient's head. This unpleasant performance takes tremendous skill. Lice are surprisingly agile and nits all but invisible. The only comfort was the common ground I shared with the woman in whose hair I was clumsily ferreting around. She was as unwilling to be deprived, arbitrarily, of the parasitic property, as I was to perform the service.

Another trying chore was to wash, several times a day, with the aid of a professional nurse, a man who I was positive was already dead during the time we were doubling him up to sponge his back, and then straightening him out again. It was three days before the rest of the staff agreed with my prognosis. I *presume* they were in the right, since rigor mortis had failed to set in during the period that I had dealt with him. I never have understood why we should be so spotlessly clean to go into our coffins.

My father gave up Edmondthorpe in 1939 and we moved to a house in Cadogan Square. On the outbreak of war he rejoined the army and was allotted the duties of military quartering commandment. His first posting was to Melton Mowbray. So back to Leicestershire we went, to a hired hunting box, in the town, called Warwick Lodge. The next station up the line was Brooksby. Brooksby Hall was a military convalescent home. I caught the train there every morning at 8 am and back again at 2 pm. The rest of the day was my own. The boredom was excruciating. I had a bicycle, but there is a limit to how far one can cycle on an ice-cold winter's afternoon. The winter of 1939—40 was unprecedented in its severity. When I asked, just once, if I might borrow the car, my mother replied, as though spelling the obvious out to an idiot, that the petrol ration was insufficient for *her* needs.

The atmosphere at Brooksby of lonely, equally bored, giggling girls was no more conducive to fulfillment. One also felt that, when the privation, let alone the danger, of others, was so much greater then one's own, to attempt to change one's circumstances would be everything that was discreditable.

To my enormous relief, Brooksby closed down within two years. Just before it did, I threw in my lot with two cousins from Hertfordshire, who were going to work in the transport department of Percival Aircraft Ltd, which manufactured parts for aeroplanes, at what is now Luton Airport. A letter to me from a fellow V.A.D. nurse at Brooksby sums up the feelings of the segregated female population of the period.

> ... I see no reason why we should all lose contact with you, because even though total war wages throughout these islands, there is still the medium of post, and the railway, so we must hope for better days and more opportunity to see one's friends. I am supposed to be going to London to see my brother March 18–23rd. I suppose there would be no chance of you being let loose on the Metropolis then? I had to show your letter to Matron and she said to convey her love and that her incredulity exceeds her belief that you have a reputation as a hard worker; it's only because you are in a job where you can't lock yourself in the loo all day long.
>
> Far from increasing my desire for work, like the present situation seems to have done yours, I find myself feeling less and less like work every day; in fact I very much doubt if the personal presence of a Hun soldier would even get me into frenzied activity. We hear from Nurse Elizabeth Grant-Williams now and then and she is daily expecting invasion at her new post at the Gog Magog Convalescent Home, which seems to be in the firing line. Unlike me she feels very defiant and puts at the end of her letter 'I'll see the Germans don't get past me.'
>
> I hope you have good news of Mark. Do you know Anthony Abel-Smith is missing in Libya? If you ask me it is a perfectly bloody life and I can't see any hope of it getting better for some time.

These words were penned on March 7, 1942.

At the factory we were desperately anxious that nobody should suspect what our background was. I cannot think why. Had we been true to ourselves, we should not have been bothering about it either way. I worked hard because I had nothing else to do and was responsible only to myself. On one occasion I was approached by a Union man and told to slow down as, by comparison, I was making the lads look as if they were shirking. I acted thick and explained I only knew one way to work and would not be able to learn any other.

We three drove small vans to the depots in the town and to Wrest and Luton Hoo, both in Bedfordshire. There were no sign-posts. But there were no roundabouts, either. It proved not as difficult to find our way, without direction aids, as we had feared. I always picked up any hitch-hiker (mostly soldiers), a thing I would not dare to do nowadays.

The lorry drivers lived in perpetual fear of being called up. They were pleasant and friendly, but not a gallant band. They did a not inconsiderable amount of furniture moving during working hours. The transport manager, who was as crafty as any of them, became very anxious on one occasion when a driver was long overdue, returning from a run. When the man did, at length, appear, it transpired that there had been some trouble with a piano, which had got wedged on the stairs that the gang was considerately carrying it up.

There was one Jewish worker. He performed the humble job of sweeping the factory floor. His mates were very pleasant to him to his face, and very insulting about him behind his back. I went to an intelligent man called Bob Slater—I think he was a progress chaser—and said there appeared to be no reason behind this unpleasant behaviour, so what was it about? Bob Slater said that there was every reason. Jews were not to be trusted. They came into a district, set up shop and undercut all the local traders.

"So what?" I said, "two can play that game." Not against Jews, I was told. A whole family would be content to live in one room until they had made their way. No respectable Englishman would be prepared to live like that.

I have referred to the lorry drivers without much praise. There was, in fact, one among them who remains the only saint that I have ever met. He was somewhat ill-favoured in appearance. I never caught him in a peevish or ill-tempered mood. Always he was calm, kindly, sympathetic; more than ready to take on extra work, do the job that nobody fancied: all as a matter of course. He never looked for thanks nor asked for a return favour. The only positive thing about him was that he seemed in mortal dread of his wife. I formed a very adverse opinion of this woman who could not possibly have anything to complain of. I then met her and quickly realised that that was precisely her problem.

She was good-looking, outgoing, friendly and intelligent. Reading between the lines it was easy to understand how difficult it is to live with somebody who never answers back; meets one submissively half way in a cantankerous outburst; whose angelic nature leaves the partner with an unshared sense of guilt for all the tormented moods that the average individual is prone to. The place for true saints is indeed on the top of a pillar or, out of range of human tantrums, in a desert. Human nature being what it is, small wonder that saints get stoned or stuck full of arrows.

The middle class turn of mind found the topsy-turvy element of wartime life difficult to come to terms with, as a letter I received from Brenda in March 1942 demonstrates.

What snobs Jane's friends are not to take the Yanks out — I should have gone out with the Yanks — *much* more fun. I didn't think the tone of your letter hearty. My friend Angela Post and sister are in the Auxiliary Fire Service and seem miserable. The sister was really rather absurd — because she complained the A.F.S. were such awful people — no one to speak to — and only *one* had been to *Harrow*!! I said the others must have been vastly nicer and she seemed to think me quite mad. She also said that when the A.F.S. were playing a game of saying what they would be doing if they could, such as 'being at the flicks' or 'going to sleep' or 'at the P. de D.' the Posts said 'we wish we were at the Berkeley!', which of course was not at all well received by the others.

Brenda was, herself, very anxious about finding some not uncongenial job. At an interview she asked (hopefully?) whether prostitutes were exempt and was told that, in some cases, they were; which she thought very odd.

One friendship we made at Percivals lasted until after the end of the War. The young man in charge of the petrol pumps and supply, Alf Taylor, was, in civvy street, a cockney barrow boy. In his character I explored not an alien culture — the demarcation of its guidelines rather resembled that of my own in its unwritten rules — but a distinct race of individualist, hitherto unknown to me. He taught me a great deal of rhyming slang, which I have remembered, and some sentences of Yiddish, which I have forgotten.

Alf had been drafted into the West Kent Regiment, in which he had served for six months before being invalided out with tubercular symptoms. Like my brother, John, whose bad eyesight barred him from active service, he felt a strong sense of rejection and of being washed up like so much jetsam; especially since his brothers, Red Ted and Ritchie, inculcated their own rich cockney pattern of events which almost certainly had not happened, in their letters home.

Ritchie was not, as you may be supposing, short for Richard. On the day his son was born, Mr Taylor senior had won a lot of money by backing an outside chance called 'Rich Gift'. . . . Fortunately the priest whose office it was to christen the child had, in common with most of his colleagues in the Church of England, not been one to ask questions or acquaint himself in any way with his parishioners. He had congratulated the parents on their obvious awareness of the blessing of the Almighty, in His bestowel on them of a son.

The West Kent Regiment more sincerely deserves to be congratulated in that, within the space of six months, they had inculcated a deep sense of regimental pride and loyalty into this unlikely service material.

"My regiment," Alf informed me, "is the oldest in the British Army."

"When was it raised?" I asked, taking a genuine interest. A

date was named some time within the last fourteen years of the 17th century.

"Then it's not," I stated, "the Grenadiers are older than that." I was not prepared for the riposte: "Damn you, Urs, I didn't think you'd know."

In 1943 Alf left Percivals and returned to a market fruit stall in Islington. I ended the war as a filing clerk in the War Office. The department was full of girls who felt they were worthy of better things. Foremost in this category was a young woman who made great play with two features of her background: 1. that she had been Tom Driberg's secretary; 2 that her full title was the Hon. Mrs Latham. She made no friends on either count. I had difficulty in memorising a telephone number that I often needed to use. She told me: "It's easy. One three eight one: the date of the Peasants' Revolt." Of course *I* knew the date of the Peasants' Revolt, but I was astonished that she did. In retrospect, of course, she would know. And I am amazed that she took it for granted that I did.

Alf and I corresponded. The following letter demonstrates the inbred determination of both our cultures not to be put upon by bureaucracy, even when there is no vital need to make a stand.

Many thanks for the letter you sent me. I was wondering if you had forgotten me. Well here's a bit of what I'm doing, trade is not too bad, but I am sorry to say I cannot get the stuff, now here is a bit of your old Alf talking. When I first went back to the stall, I made an application for a tomato alication thinking it was a walk over for me to get and was very surprised when I got turned down, anyway I went back to the office and asked why, they told me the reason was because the license was in my mother's name and as she had been away so long they could not grant it, but said that if I could get the license altered into my name I could get it, well to cut it short I asked to go in front of the committee which they granted, well the day arrived to go to the meeting, and me thinking that all there would be there would be a couple of old boys, but to my *utter amazement* there was a big room with a very large round table and about twenty men sitting round it, I had not sat down in the chair when up got the chairman, 'ah Mr Taylor' he said, 'you want to know why you have failed in your application' and he rattled off about the license being in mum's name, and why did I not get it changed to my name after he had finish I started I said 'gentlemen, my mother has had that stall ever since she was married, my father had it put in her name so that if anything happened to him she always had something to hearn her daily bread,' then up would jump another mug and say all we ask you to do is alter the license into your name, so I turn to him and said, 'what difference does it make whether it is in my old mother's name or mine they would all be sold on the same stall, anyway who is more entitled to the alication than my mother who has eight sons in the forces and who the doctor has given only a few months to live it would be like stabbing her in the back to take away her only piece of independence she as, if that is what you could do to you mother, well then I can't.' After my speech they were mumbling to one another, up got the chairman and told me I would hear the results in a few days, in which I did, I had been granted an alication, and I am the only *man* who has got one without a food license.

The eight sons in the forces and the mother with only a few months to live was deliberately pitching it almost too steep, since the glee of getting away with it was thus intensified.

I recollect the declaration of War in 1939 as almost a relief. Europe had been waiting for it for over a year and, as the play had to be performed, it was time the curtain went up.

The second thing I recall is being distinctly relieved that I was still a virgin. Every hoarding carried information as to the number and names of the venereal diseases it was possible to contract, followed by explicit details of the symptoms. Great was my astonishment to realise that I had had every symptom of all the venereal diseases for as long as I could remember. It left me feeling not a little uneasy. Thinking the matter over dispassionately I told myself, thankfully, that in this particular game of chance I could afford to pass.

The following letters have been selected as examples of a need for mutual bonding in the face of a common crisis which was going to persist for who knew how long. Before the War I had not carried on a regular correspondence with any of the friends here represented. Primarily we wrote to amuse each other and to exchange social gossip of a kind that we would have been in close touch with, were we not isolated in various parts of England, France and later North Africa and even farther afield. The actual War scene is seldom mentioned. That was for the newspapers and the radio. Letters were a blessed interruption of the tension of our lives.

In these extracts I am grateful to the dramatic element in the epistolary style of Major Bruce Shand MC which, by heightening them, epitomises more readily the problems we were all facing and which are difficult to recall accurately in hindsight.

A surprising number of my letters mention 'Rags', a mongrel bitch which I had got from the Battersea Dogs' Home. I have a letter from my father which contains a message of love for Rags and the nostalgic reflection that he had not seen her for two years. The fact that he had not seen his only daughter for the same amount of time passes unregretted; it is Rags who gets his love. She *was* a very delightful dog.

I appear to have kept no letters concerning the death of my brother at El Alamein, which is very surprising and inexplicable. I kept every other letter, and some of them are very dull.

The first letter illustrates the fate of many men who entered one of the services intending to make it their profession, found that the actuality was not what they had expected, got their discharge, and then were clawed back by the talons of war. The writer was a nephew of the notorious Irish patriot, the Countess Markowitz. His family lived at Lissadell, County Sligo, and also owned what the writer humorously referred to as the Summer Palace, a red brick villa, of appalling chaos and discomfort, on the seafront at Bundoran.

From Brian Gore-Booth, Su. Lt. R.N.R., H.M.S. Exmouth.
Postmarked 14 January 1940. Received from H.M. Ships.

> Your letter was received with interest. The knowledge that I
> have subscribed a little mirth to the Wyndham homestead helps
> to sustain me, I can assure you. Of particular interest were your

comments on Unity Mitford and a fuller report would be appreciated. Not much gossip comes my way now, and any titbits about people I know does much to cheer me on my watery way! The Nazis show signs of being increasingly tiresome which is rather a bore for anyone who appears to so utterly lack the heroic spirit as I do. That old 'grin and bear it' attitude seems to be entirely lacking, especially when one knows that people like your brother Henry are hunting two days a week and shooting at weekends. Really it is remarkable how lucky some people are. I think I will become a socialist...

The prospect of ever getting leave here is as remote as ever, it seems the only people who understand the meaning of the word are the army.

Well, they say the darkest hour is before the dawn, so I must hope that the sun of happiness is about to burst upon me any day now. Hoping your prospects are somewhat less bleak than mine.

I replied on January 20th:

As soon as I received your letter, sparing neither trouble nor expense, I wrote to John to ask for further news of Miss Mitford. I think I can do no better than send you his reply in the sincere hope that it will lighten, if only for a few moments, the drab darkness of your daily drudgery.

On 23 January 1940, H.M.S. *Exmouth* was torpedoed with the loss of all on board. My letter and John's were returned to me stamped 'Return to Sender. Admiralty instructions.'

I wish I could quote from John's gloomily funny account of Unity Mitford, but John stipulated that whereas I might cheer up Brian with the story, it was on no account to be used for any conversational purpose since it had been confided to him by Unity's sister Debo.

From Bruce Shand, 'A' Squadron, 12th Royal Lancers, BEF.
30 December 1939.

It was charming of you to send me that spirited sporting card and all that exciting information about your dear father and the devilment at Melton. I should like to thrill you and make your flesh creep with tales of daring do from the 'front' or even send you a captured 'pickel haube' but, as you probably know, Britain's thirsting bloodhounds have not yet had a chance to bid for glory and I for one, am content to remain quite passive.

My military duties have not been too arduous as they have been confined to looking after the food and comforts of my brother officers. Each morning sees me in the nearest market town bickering and fighting in the 'Halles' over the price of a moribund tomato and talking what I am afraid is very filthy argot. But as you know I am not the man to spare myself, and three weeks ago I was stricken with 'flu and have only just moved from my bed, having been in a *very bad state.* So bad, in fact, that I am being sent on Monday to Cannes for a complete rest, which of course is only right. I expect I shall be feted as *un pauvre blessé.*

You cannot imagine how utterly boring it is here, because altho' we are quite comfortable, there is nothing to do except eat and drink and enlarge one's already replete liver. I read and write more than I have ever done — with the invention of the telephone one was inclined to forget the latter art (I write this rather with my tongue in my cheek) . . .

How are those good boys, your brothers? I am glad Mark is in good spirits and pulling quips at the army. Has Henry gone abroad yet 'with his father's sword behind him'? Remember me to them and say I have my back to the wall.

It is related that when a brother officer said to Lieutenant Shand on the beaches of Dunkirk? 'I don't think God is on our side this time, do you?' he received the chilling reply: 'I couldn't really say. I am not very well acquainted with the gentleman.'

From Bruce Shand, 12th R. Lancers, Dorking.
30 November 1940.

This may be the last letter you may get from me (unless I can contrive to send you a message from some astral plane), as tomorrow we set forth on some kind of military manoeuvre lasting four days and nights and with apparently no break for sleep or other refreshments. I cannot tell you how cold it is — already some of the machines are refusing to work — rot

their guts. Already I sense the subsequent sick bed and the
nodding of funeral plumes.

I would have written before now but have been engaged in
maddening social activity that has at last, praise Heaven, abated.
A few of us in our youthful exuberance decided to give a cocktail
party 'for our friends' (I don't know who the Hell mine are). The
next thing I overhear is the wife of the Colonel remarking to one
of her cronies 'isn't it wonderful, we (mark this pronoun) are
having a cocktail party in the Mess (collapse of me behind an
adjacent hedgerow) and dear Bruce is arranging it all' (Ave
Maria!).

So there it was and I spent maddened days trying to buy all
the ridiculous things that are for some reason so essential to the
success of these entertainments. Needless to say they were quite
unobtainable. However it passed 'without incident', as the
communiqués so originally say of the most devastating air
raids — but its memory and the attendant horrors have, with
the prospect of these Spartan nights, deranged my lazy acceptance
of life not a little!

Otherwise things could not be duller — we are all rather
scared as they are starting to change around this part of the army
a bit and none of us know what is going to happen to us . . . .

I have no letters of the slightest general interest for the first half
of 1941 other than Bruce Shand's highly individual account of life
on this beleaguered isle during that worryingly procrastinating
period. He was the only correspondent who ventured to contem-
plate the future.

From Bruce Shand, at Charlwood, Surrey. 12 March 1941.

. . . Most of the few friends I had have gone away. There is a
mass of youth, refreshing but a trifle overwhelming at times![1]
What can the end of all this be? I must confess that I am
infinitely more interested in the psychological and social results
than in any economic and political eventualities. Don't you

---

[1] Bruce Shand was 24 years old.

think that we shall witness some very strange anomalies before we are much older? One of the few advantages of the war seems to be that it is releasing people of the many inhibitions that are the inevitable lot of a class-conscious race like the British (*made* class conscious thro' a political system) and really is enabling them to express their personalities.

I do think that if the right democratic medium is fixed afterwards we shall have an infinitely happier and more intelligent social order. Also the 'Society' (odious word — I use it *faute de mieux*) element will no longer be an expression of wealth but of culture and wit. Anyway it is an attractive ideal which I hope may materialize — and you may have your salon yet!

I have read singularly little lately that is worthy of mentioning to you. I think you would like Miss Booth's[1] book — anyway you *ought* to read it (I get wild with rage when anyone said this to me) tho' it's a trifle too 'slick'.

Have you ever read *Les Liaisons Dangereuses* by Choderlos de Laclos? It is a somewhat salacious but charmingly satirical French classic — practically unknown in this country owing to the prudery of our forebears. There is a good translation — if you can't get it let me know as I have a black let book shop that would get the original Koran if one gave them sufficient time! . . . . .

In many ways the hope of a future access to culture and wit on a wider level than the writer of the preceding letter hoped for has indeed been fulfilled, but in its train stalks pretension of a peculiarly pitiable kind: the wearers of Old Etonian ties who feel the need to advertise their seat of education in case, horrid thought, it might not be universally recognised; their parents, who ape the most tedious conventions of upper class entertaining before the Wars — and manage to get it just wrong anyhow!

The next letter, from the eldest of the Cole sisters of Florence Court, demonstrates the pattern in which the old-fashioned concept of domestic service was crumbling and the hitherto waited-on were finding it less hassle to wait on themselves.

---

[1] Claire Booth, later married Henry Luce.

From Ann, wife of J. H. James of the Admiralty. 31 May 1941.

You once kindly warned me against Brenda's ex-nurse; there is now another name to be added to the black list — Eva Andrew, whom I have sacked with ignominy. When she first came she was kind and obliging but suddenly turned into a fiend directly I had a good and efficient maid here, and became jealous of her and determined to oust her but got ousted herself! I am now looking after Michael myself until I find another and better nurse. Are you still finding your work very irksome? I am going to run the penny a week scheme for the Red Cross in this village (Ashampstead) but so far have been too busy being nursemaid to do anything about it.

Did you see the gloomy details of a police case involving Gertrude Miller Mundy and some unscrupulous young man who had been fleecing her? I think it must be Aunt Mollie as there is only one lot of *Miller* Mundy's — ask the F[emale] P[arent]. Peter [Miller Mundy]'s wife is having a baby in November and Aunts Pry and Bun can think of nothing else — great auntdom has rushed on them and left them breathless. I don't think I have any exciting news but do write and tell me your doings."

From Bruce Shand, XII Royal Lancers, Tidworth. 11 July 1941.

Forgive me for not writing before but the strain and heat of the last few days have been prodigious. Now at last it is pouring with rain and a gloomy collection of people sit in a steaming tent with even less expression than usual on their heavy faces, listening to the thunder. Do you dislike the heat as much as I do? Somehow I find it difficult to imagine a heat wave in Melton but no doubt it is quite possible.

Life in most places in England must be more than dull at present but I cannot help feeling that we possess the quintessence of ennui and tedium in this establishment. I cannot but feel Mark[1] must be bored stiff but he never seems to show it and always makes me laugh even in the midst of exhausting and apparently timeless afternoons.

---

[1] My youngest brother, whose boredom threshold has always been high.

Surely this endless sitting about, being issued with the wrong equipment, and other muddles that so typify the British War Effort, must be far the worst part of the struggle?

Maybe one is the child of the wrong generation and consequently likes seeing people and changes all the time and therefore this all seems infinitely worse — but whatever the cause the effect is quite intolerable! The only thing that has consoled me is the fact that Beaverbrook and Bush are receiving the most awful pounding from the Press and Parliament, which is delightful . . . . . .

This is a crazy dispirited letter which I hope you'll excuse — am afraid a lot of mine are but I find it almost impossible to make any sense at the moment.

The only thing I've read is called *The Earth Is The Lord's*, all about Ghengis Khan but far too full of steppes and mares' milk and the like. I don't recommend it.

From Bruce Shand at Tidworth. 9 August 1941

. . . . Thank Heaven I retire to the quiet of the New Forest tomorrow to stay with my mother who I am sorry to say is showing a very poor spirit about Mrs Clifton Brown's charitable schemes. I am vastly impressed at the zest with which you have entered into these activities . . . .

As far as I remember, the Colonel's wife's scheme was that the officers' wives or mothers should write regularly to the wives of the men and keep Mrs Clifton Brown posted as to the results. Bruce's mother was not the only one not to enter into this scheme with zest: Mark's mother showed a similar lack of enthusiasm. Therefore Mark's sister found herself corresponding with about six very nice women whose husbands were serving in 'B' squadron of the 12th Royal Lancers. As soon as the correspondence had got well under way the Army, for its own inscrutable reasons, moved Mark to another squadron. To quote a favourite expression of Shand's at the time: Oh, the folly of it all! I still, by chance, retain one letter from the many I exchanged with unknowm women whose lives the fortunes of War had crossed with mine. I quote in full.

ASTRIDE THE WALL

From Frances Revens, 31 Irving Road, Coventry. 26 October 1942.

Please forgive the delay in writing to you in answer to your letter of the 30th September. Nevertheless I was very pleased to receive it. My mail has dropped off instead of speeding up since it is now nearly six weeks since I received any news whatever.

When I went to the 'At Home' in London I had hopes that I should meet you there and was greatly disappointed when I heard that you were unable to attend. Still, perhaps better luck next time! I am so pleased to learn that you are getting news through so quickly from your brother . . . . The newsletter this last time was very good indeed and I have sent it on to my husband hoping that he will have the luck to receive it.

I have not yet begun fire-watching and I cannot say I relish the idea of doing it, but then I never was very brave. You have more pluck than I have to have been doing it for this length of time.[1] Good luck and God bless you in your good work. I am sure one of these days He will reward you for all you have done when this great trial is over and victory ours.

It is a very clever, tactful idea of Gen. Montgomery and his hat with the regimental badges.

Do write again as soon as you can for your letters do a great deal to cheer me up, especially in this time of worry. Now the fighting has again started in Egypt it will be harder still to keep one's chin up, but we must for the sake of our dear ones out there. God bless you and keep you safe always.

This moving letter demonstrates the unfortunate side of corresponding with wives whose husbands were in a different squadron to that my brother was serving in: I was hearing from Mark; Mrs Revens was receiving no news. Mark did ask me to write to the wife of his soldier servant in his new squadron, who was called Ron Boyden, came from Lavenham, Suffolk, and is described by my brother as resembling 'a small cherub'. I regret that no letters from the cherub's wife survive.

---

[1] I can't remember ever fire-watching. I suppose there was a rota. I also blush for the impression Mrs Revens gained about how hard I was working. It arose from a wish to exchange experiences.

142

WAR CORRESPONDENCE

From Bruce Shand, 12th Lancers, Westbury. 3 September 1941.

A very sinister date, I fear, on which to write to you. Incredible
to think this curious existence has only lasted two dreary little
years — I feel it is at least ten since I heard those brave words of
Mr Chamberlain's.

The 3rd September has always been cropping up in history.
Oliver Cromwell, I fancy, was born, died and fought his greatest
battle (Worcester) on that particular day of the month. Several
other things happened too but I cannot remember what at the
moment!

Mark, as you say, is wildly excited about going abroad and I
only wish I could share his enthusiasm, but I think that *'partant
pour la Syrie'* is essentially a pristine joy!

What I dread most, apart from flies and dust, is the thought
that we may be stuck there for years after the War, which would
be utterly damnable! Oh, how I dislike the confusion of packing
and equipping oneself for a campaign in the East (or anywhere
else for that matter) and making final financial arrangements
(necessarily somewhat exiguous these days) and Heaven know
what else besides.

From Ann James, Ashampstead, Reading. 20 November 1941.

I thought I had told you that Aunt Molly had been writing
indiscreet letters to some dogfoot man and then employed a
crook to get the letters back; the crook got immense sums of
money from her on false pretences and so she sued him. Stories
appeared in the press of scenes in the man's flat — Aunt Molly
slapping his face (the crook's) — his defence said that Aunt
Molly's evidence was unreliable as she was well known to be a
woman who made scenes in public places, also that she was old
enough to be the young man's mother, if not grandmother! Poor
Uncle Godfrey [Miller Mundy] is in a horrid way, what with his
ex-wife's performance, and Angela [his daughter] has also dis-
tinguished herself and her name is not mentioned at the moment,
but the reason is still obscure; my informant is Aunt Bun, so not
only must the proverbial grain of salt be swallowed, but the
whole cruet as well!

Uncle G.'s German lady, Ullu, has a much younger and

more attractive sister, whose German husband is interned in Canada. This sister was asked to shoot at Red Rice [Godfrey's house in Hampshire] and so captivated a member of the syndicate, who was supposed to be inconsolable on the death of his wife, eight months ago, that he asked the German to marry him and she at once sent a cable to Canada, asking for a divorce!

From John Wyndham at Warwick Lodge, Melton Mowbray.
6 September 1941.

This is to thank you for the slippers you are going to give me. They are the nicest kind of slipper there is and I am very grateful. When I return to London I will send you the ration book with margarine coupons in it. I return tomorrow, which is glum.

Mr Bryant turned up here last night.

He had walked all the way from Nottingham, having failed to obtain a single lift (he tried to stop two cars but they sped on heartlessly). He arrived at 2 am, soaked to the skin.

Joan has been took bad and has been sent home to her ma.

The food gets worse and worse. The fish pie last night tasted of dirty harbour. Whiteley[1] says the cook's a bit nuts and the servants are getting restive because the food they are getting is almost uneatable.

Lunch with Sir Raymond [Greene] the other day. Grouse. And real cream. Mr Edward Greene announced that he had seen Aunt Maggie in Gloucestershire with Queen Mary and that Aunt Maggie looked stunning in strawberry pink.

Queen Mary, visiting Bath one day, came upon a number of Canadian soldiers. They asked for her autograph and she gave it to them. Then she agreed that one of them might photograph her and, just as the photograph was being taken, those closest to her suddenly put their arms round her waist. This was embarrassing, but Queen Mary was quite amused although afterwards she was heard to complain because old Coke [her equerry] had done nothing to stop it. But what could Coke do? He could hardly slap the offending hands and say sharply: 'Now, now, lay off our Queen!'

---

[1] Whiteley, my parents' parlour maid, in her 40s made a wartime marriage with Mr Bryant, an RAF flier, who was almost immediately killed.

Maxine Birley has announced her intention of becoming a doctor. She is coming to London to be a medical student. She begins her studies at, I believe, St Mary's Hospital for Incurables. Which strikes me as being an ambitious start.

Apocryphal story. A newly formed unit of soldiers was as yet unequipped, so they went on a field day armed only with broom sticks. They were told that if they said 'Bang' it would be understood for the purposes of the mock battle they were to wage that they were letting off a rifle. 'Bang-Bang' would represent a machine gun. 'Swish' would mean a bayonet.

A rather small and down-trodden private's position was in a wood. Presently a large and superior soldier on the side of the enemy appeared. So the little private said 'Bang' as loud as he could. The enemy continued to advance. The little private this time tried bigger stuff and cried 'Bang-Bang.' Still the enemy came on, until, when he was quite close, the little private, in desperation, said 'Swish.' To his amazement the enemy did not pause but walked right past him.

'Stop!' cried the little private, by this time much annoyed. 'Your dead. I went Bang, Bang-Bang *and* Swish.'

'Silly,' said his adversary as he disappeared into the under-growth. 'Didn't you hear me say Chug-Chug? I'm a tank.'

From Brenda, née Alexander, wife of Michael Maclagan, Intelligence. November 1941.

What adventures you are having — it sounds fun. I'm so glad Rags is with you. I have just been for an interview. I *hope* I shall hear no more, but one can't tell. The woman was quite nice. She had a sense of humour — I was lucky to get her as the others looked like mad governesses (probably were). I am so tired I can't write much more. It's all so upsetting — a new helper at the Red Cross (only afternoons), 23 years old — has never been interviewed!

From my mother at Melton Mowbray. 16 December 1941.

I enjoyed your letter so much. What really bad luck that your van should have behaved so badly on your first long journey.

145

Sickening . . . . I enclose Mark's letter which arrived yesterday. I
was rather disappointed to see the date was 29 *Oct* and this
morning came an airgraph, obviously from Cairo. But Mark
doesn't date it!! Exasperating I find it. The 'Dicky'[1] Mountbattens
have just reached this country from U.S.A. where he'd gone to
from Crete with some battered remains of ships to be mended.
They flew with their 18-year old daughter to Lisbon, then found
only two possible places on the plane for England. Ld and Ly
came on, leaving Miss MB alone in Portugal where she will be
for the Duration, as now an edict has gone forth not allowing
anyone to travel by air *anywhere*. Lord Dicky, it seems, was
consulted by the American Admiralty as to what he'd advise as
to the disposition of the American Fleet, in view of the Threat of
Japan and War — and he said *whatever* they did not to keep the
ships together in Harbour but to keep Cruising to and fro — the
American Admiralty answered 'the Boys like being altogether'
and disregarded all he said. One wonders whether the 'Boys' like
it so much now? What are left of them . . .

My mother's excitement at passing on this titbit can be gauged
by her lavish use of capital letters to highlight the drama.

From Brenda Maclagan in London. December 1941.

Today I have arranged to leave the Ministry; I hope you won't
think me a miserable shirker — but it really was too much. I
now weigh less than 7 stone and I have the curse almost all the
time. I am going to a doctor before I melt away. I feel and look
like nothing human. I don't think I would do either myself or
the Ministry any good by staying on — and also the Boss was a
great trial — he was very nice,, but like so many, he did not
know where to stop. Please don't go and repeat it although I
know it's funny. How are your 'wives'? Write to me.

---

[1] The inverted commas are an acknowledgement that as my mother did not
know the Mountbattens she had no business calling him Dicky. She was
something of a lion hunter and very competitive with her eldest sister-in-law,
Violet Leconfield.

The members of the M.E.F. wrote in pencil unless they were in Cairo or Alexandria. Some of the following letters have been very difficult to decipher.

From Bruce Shand, 12th Lancers, M.E.F. 5 June 1942.

Your airgraph arrived on the eve of Waterloo and since then until today we have been far too active for one of peaceful tastes like myself — and not nearly enough sleep which I find almost worse than anything — the night never seems to last more than three or four hours and then is often beset with alarums. Mark is out somewhere in the desert looking for Germans — periodically his voice comes through over the wireless (beside which I am writing this), not, as you might expect, with news of enemy activity — but much more frequently with social gossip: 'Oh hello — I've just met old So-and-So who asked to be remembered to you; he tells me that he's just heard from England that B. is getting a divorce', and so on, which makes me laugh.

Graceless boy — he put up a fearful exhibition the other morning. Just prior to this present conflict I thought that my Squadron was in need of some form of ghostly consolation and accordingly engaged the services of a priest who undertook a celebration of some forty minutes.

He was a well-meaning but would-be unconventional man and spurned the bivouac which I placed at his disposal in which to change, but instead chose to robe before the mute and assembled congregation who stared aghast at his Lacoon-like writhings with his surplice in the high wind.

Being finally arrayed he suddenly said, 'Now somebody choose an hymn!' We were all completely stunned by this request. I felt I should do something but my mind became a void and I was wondering what was going to happen when Mark said very firmly: 'No. 8' — thank God, I thought, for a boy with enterprise, and duly opened the book. To my horror No. 8 was a completely obscure piece of verse (so it seemed) appointed for the Churching of Women or other interesting function. 'One, two, three' said the padre, 'and when I drop my finger we'll all begin'. What an optimist — nothing happened, except that I started off on this unknown ocean of song in a quavering voice,

determined to make some kind of effort (in which I was not
joined for three lines) while Master Wyndham had an appalling
fit of suppressed giggles. Oh the shame of it all, Ursula. I
condemned him to look after the padre and he so far lost his
nerve as to ask him to stay to lunch at 10.30 am!

He has really been awfully good lately — all the troop
leaders have had a very trying time and he is never depressed and
always in a good humour — surely God's great gift.

[*Written in ink*] Since writing this we have had every kind of
excitement and divertissement and are now back in Cairo —
really rather weary and I must confess that I am glad to see the
place altho' it is stinking hot. Things really have been rather
hectic lately and moving swiftly — much more like (or far too
much like) France two years ago.

I am not at all prepared for post-War reconstruction, are
you? Where do we all fit in? What a prospect.

The next letter is from Henry, on his way to North Africa,
written to our mother. The mysterious reference to 'Aunt Maggie's
boss' can be taken to convey the information that he was travelling
on the *Queen Mary*. (Our Aunt Maggie held the post of one of the
women of the bedchamber, to give her her precise title, and was
full of the rigours of life at Badminton.) The other oblique reference
is to South Africa. Our Uncle Hugh had emigrated there in the
early 1900s.

Dear Mummy,
We should reach port the day after tomorrow so I am dashing
off a quick letter to you. We have had a very comfortable
voyage except it is far too crowded but it should not be for
long. We are now getting to the really hot weather and I can
see a few unpleasant days ahead. It is the worst time of the
year to be in this part of the world.

I have a comfortable cabin which I share with another guy
by name John Watts, very nice, he was at Winchester, but a
bit too serious. The cabin was a single one in peace time.
Being a bright boy I offered him the top bunk. He jumped at
it and only realised when he got into bed that I had the lush
original bed and he had a bunk put over it. Aunt Maggie's

boss has been all one would expect, of course it's altered but on the whole I think I am lucky. Not much other news I can tell. I am looking forward to seeing Uncle Hugh's country again and hope we stay there awhile. It is the best time of year to be there as well.
Love, Henry.

From Mark Wyndham, XII R. Lancers. 10 September 1942.

Dear Miss Wyndham, I received your letter of June 30th. The Major received one too. On receipt of your letter I have just repulsed Rommel's strong attempt to break the Alamein line. I am now starting on a campaign of super self-propaganda in order that mothers, etc., can hold their own with other mothers, whose sons are apparently less modest and security-minded than myself. I have just read a *Daily Sketch* of June 16th, speaking of the great tank struggle in dust and heat and the roaring of guns and shells; all this I have never mentioned. Mummy met Lady Colquoun, who had a letter from Ivor stating he was *watching* the battle as he wrote. It goes without saying that every letter I write I have to jump into shell holes four or five times during writing to avoid complete obliteration. As to watching the battle, I myself navigated a whole Brigade into action some few weeks ago (having got them there I hastily withdrew, but keep that under your hat). Not seen Henry for some time. Henry and I both think you all nincompoops not understanding about Aunt M.'s Boss. He was very uncomfortable owing to sharing her with 1,300 others. Love, Mark.

I cannot remember what induced the tone of this letter, but I, for one, wish it had been maintained.

From Ann James, Bradfield, Berks. 12 September 1942.

Your letter made me laugh a lot and I read the biblical part to Jack who chortled over it.
    I rather fancy myself on being an authority on the Old Testament and knew of the behaviour of Lot's daughters, but did *not* know of the hurly burly of the angels and the pansies. I must

149

quickly buy a Bible as I am ashamed to say this house does not possess one.

I returned from Ireland last Tuesday after a fortnight's visit. The weather was bad but it was lovely to be home in a land flowing with milk, cream and honey. Michael took a fancy to his step-grandmother and ran after her calling her Gandhi, a somewhat ironic and backhanded compliment, considering her bulk.

Aunt Kathleen [Villiers] was at home and said she had never much cared for Egghead, but that on his last visit of Florence Court she was pleasantly surprised to find him so well informed on many subjects. Alas, though, this was somewhat counterbalanced by his hoggish table manners, which have got worse with age apparently and both Aunt K. and Mary [Enniskillen]'s sole topic of conversation during the first few days I was there consisted in relating in shocked tones how Egghead had seized plum after plum; while one hand was ramming it down his throat, the other hand was reaching for another, and another time Mary watched fascinated but appalled while he stuffed his mouth so full of bread and butter that a large portion stuck out, which he then proceeded to ram in with great blows of his fist. The cream had to be kept on a different table else otherwise no one else got a look in, so, altogether, the old man is qualifying for a pig sty.

From Bruce Shand, 12th Lancers, M.E.F. 30 October 1942.

This is the letter I have been meaning to write to you for a very long time and for which late appearance I crave your indulgence. As you have probably seen we have once again all been projected into battle, but as yet have not been required to play any great part in it, which is a mercy tho' something of an anticlimax, and we are all sitting around doing singularly little. Mark, indeed, seemed so idle this morning that I presented him with a copy of Mr Churchill's *Great Contemporaries* and sent him away to read it and only hope it may be of benefit.

He, Mark, has had us all thinking lately by his graceful division of your charming sex into two classes only: 'Ladies' and 'Prostitutes'. 'Oh,' he says, 'she was a nice lady' or 'she was a delightful prostitute' — ingenious I don't doubt and certainly saving of a lot of tedious sorting into categories, but rather shocking to my conventional beliefs.

Your last letter, the one about Mrs Smyly[1], was delivered to me under heavy shell fire (heavier in fact than I cared for), but I was so intrigued by that piece of gossip that I momentarily forgot the surrounding dangers and escaped from my car to tell Ned Mann who was in the next one — and once, I think, nursed a tendresse for the lady (I suppose Mark would call her a lady?) himself.

I am afraid this vulgar piece of paper is becoming abnormally creased, but since starting it a sand storm has arisen and made everything very difficult, not to speak of a constant stream of people asking me unanswerable questions and disturbing my train of thought. I have read singularly little lately and most of it of a rather trashy nature except for a delightful chinese novel called *A Leaf in the Storm* by a gentlemen called Lin Yutang, which I find full of a most refreshing philosophy. I believe he has also written something called *The Importance of Living* which discerning people say is admirable.

Katherine of Aragon I liked immensely, but fear I have not read as widely on that period as you have. I remember well my conversation with Miss Wyndham about Queen Elizabeth — I was forced to put forward those somewhat startling theories as a kind of foil to the mass of detailed knowledge in which she was engulfing me[2] and I did not like to appear too ignorant.

The tone of the next letter from Uncle Egghead surprises me. He had been a retired Naval Captain before the War and was fortunate enough to find War work in the Navy, which makes his untypical groans the more surprising. When we were teenagers, the Cole sisters and I often discussed with Henry the likelihood of Egghead being a virgin. The girls were unanimous in supposing he

---

[1] Diana Mills, known during the 1930s as 'the Mills Bomb' on account of her sexy appearance, married a man called Smyly. After a divorce, she married, lastingly, Earl St. Aldwyn.

[2] I think B.S. must be mixing me up with some blue-stocking of his acquaintance. I have always found Queen Elizabeth too enigmatic to have an opinion on.

was. Henry told us it was most unlikely, since Egghead was a hairy man. He certainly would not have read a book written by 'some Chink'.

From A. R. Farquhar, R.N. 24 November 1942.

> I see Bruce Shand is missing. He was in Mark's regt., was he not? I have met him with Peter [Miller Mundy] several times.
> This advance is awful; so many killed. One is brutal really. As long as one's own are not involved you just don't think about it, and when they are one's outlook changes. Ragging with Henry was always one of the joys of life, it did one good.

From Wren Beryl Bruce, Westfield College, Hampstead. January 1943.

> Thank you so much for your letter which I adored getting in spite of your very gloomy prognostications about my future. But as far as I can say God willing and the Admiralty permitting I shall be in this great city for another ten days as Betty and I are both struggling to pass an M. T. course, which we are both very afraid will prove too much for either one or both of us, but for the moment we are really working quite hard and enjoying the course immensely, added to which I have fallen madly in love with one of the instructors — isn't it all too wonderful! I do *so* hope that I shall be able to see you. Betty[1] was enormously touched by your message of affection, she is an enormous tower of strength to me in this mad turmoil of tiresome women and we have a lot to laugh and grumble about together. I don't know what I'd do if she wasn't here. Anyway if nothing else is possible, do please write and tell me your news. I hope you have the best possible news of Mark and that you are not too worried about him.

In the late summer of 1942 Bruce Shand was wounded in the leg and taken prisoner. A letter to me from Mark, announcing this, proclaims that, in the advance then proceeding, they had every hope of rescuing him. This hope was not realised and Bruce

---

[1] I wish I could remember who Betty was.

was despatched to a prisoner of war camp in Germany, from which retreat he continued to report on his surroundings with his usual cynical perception.

From Bruce Shand, Offlag IX A/H, Germany. 3 February 1943.

I trust that some of my brief communications despatched to you from various parts of Mittel Europa have arrived and if they haven't I hope this will. Life here is very similar to that which I endured at school, except that here we are not compelled to play football, thank Heaven, there is a large library — tho' somewhat mixed and one finds such unlikely bedfellows as Harriette Wilson, Dorothy Sayers and Plato. But I have thrown myself into 'serious reading' (I wonder what the opposite of serious reading is?) of 18th and 19th century history which absorbs me for several hours a day and the time seems to pass at much the same pace that it always did. I refuse to learn to play chess or any other such diversion — when I confess to an aptitude for these games you will know that prison life has become too much for me! This place is in lovely country and we have a view that makes an enormous difference to one's outlook on life — nothing is more soul destroying than the perpetual sight of a brick wall or something similar. We are periodically allowed out for walks, but I am as yet debarred from this activity, because of my leg which is nearly 'sound' as our friend Miss Smith would put it. This seems a very stupid letter but cramped space produces a cramped style and as you know (to your cost probably) I always like to spread over endless untidy sheets. I look forward very much to getting my first letter from you, but am fully expecting to wait a long time. I have embarked on one activity (not without coercion) of the result of which I am very chary — namely that of "theatricals", as another generation would have put it. My last appearance as Sir Thomas Erpingham in *Henry V* (a part of importance but no great length) hardly justifies the magnitude of the one I have just been given — however I will tell you about it when I write again.

From Ann James, Bradfield, Berks. February 1943.

. . . I will probably go to Angela's wedding [to Walter Gabler], if for no other reason than to see the family stink faces; I gather that both Miller Mundy wives will attend so evidently Uncle Godfrey has less scruples than the Didi[1] who said, referring to my wedding, 'I don't mind what happens but I *will* not stand at the top of the stairs like a Turk, with a wife at either side.'

From Ann James. 9 May 1943.

Yes, I do owe you two letters — my humblest apologies. Jack and I went to Red Rice for Easter, having farmed out the boy to a baby's home in Reading. There we found Uncle G. and Ullu very pleased with each other; Peggy came down for two nights with a charming American beau in tow and the Gablers [Angela and Walter] were also there. I am sorry to say it is pronounced Gaibler not Gabbler. He is quite nice but not anything to write home about and, like most of his compatriots, is a snob [Walter was American]. Ullu told me that he was interviewing a maid for his flat and a very grand one turned up who said that she had *always* been in service with titled people, so Walter at once responded thus: 'Oh but my wife's uncle is the Earl of Enniskillen!' Having been sworn to secrecy by Ullu over this story as Uncle G. didn't want his son-in-law to become a laughing stock, Walter told the story to me himself at dinner as an example of how hard it was to get servants now.

Jack poured scorn on Olive's Cairo story and said he had heard it at his private school. Here is a story coined by some Belfast wit. Apparently the Transport Board, having gone all Golden Arrow and deluxe, now run double decker buses from Belfast to Larne to catch the boat; as they run at night they are fitted with bunks, if you please — the story goes that while going round a hairpin bend, a young man was thrown out of a top bunk and landed on one of the lower bunks on top of an old woman who said 'Where are you going, young man?', he replied 'I am going to Larne' — 'Well, ye're not going to larn on me!' was the answer.

---

[1] The Coles' name for their father.

154

Aunt Kathleen is released from bondage as her old mother-in-law has died aged 91 so she has beetled off to Florence Court on a long visit.

From Mark Wyndham, RAC Base Depot, M.E.F. 6 April 1943.

Came out of hospital yesterday and have come here to await some employment in a base job. I am now officially termed a 'base wallah' or 'Gaberdine swine' (old jokes of the east). I went to see Gold Rush last night. I laughed once or twice but it is too old to revise. I went with Silky Sparkes who was so Drunk by the time we got to the cinema that it looked as if I would have to carry him out half-way through. Fortunately he got his finger caught in the seat and either the pain or the loss of blood (which is pure alcohol in his case) sobered him up and we came home safely; all jolly fine chaps in the XIIth! I must ring up Frances [Cole] and get her out. She usually sits and stews in her abode under the shadow of the pyramids. I can't say I have ever seen her out with any strange man, much as I would like to start some gossip. I am taking out one of the hospital sisters on Thursday. She was the head night sister and is well over thirty. It is jolly decent of me to do it, that's all. No ulterior motives at all.

From Ann James, Bradfield, Berks. 10 April 1943.

Many thanks for your letter and Egghead's which interested me for various reasons. First, Frances — I agree that she had some cause for complaint as one does tend to get grumpy if one is hauled over the coals but it all does show that she *has* changed, as we have noticed from her letters. Though Mark does not seem to have noticed much difference, does he?

A thought has just struck me that perhaps you and I and Egghead have never grown up and F. has?!! In which case I prefer the Peter Pan state!

I read your letter first so stunned by your mention of the Didi's advice but then read Egghead's letter and the matter was partially explained, though the Didi has said *nothing* on the subject to me. I admit that the idea comes into my head three times daily after meals though if I did anything about it at all I would have proper divorce and not mess about with a separation — so typical of the Didi to think of that as a sop to respectability! However I will probably do nothing about it as things are quite difficult enough without alienating J. any further as he would try and get full possession of the boy. And now a word of warning — have you mentioned the matter to Gladys?[1] If so, please contradict it as if J. thinks the Didi is working against him there will be the devil to pay. Tell her this if necessary.

I have heard from Aunt Kathleen that Hugh Gore-Booth has been killed on active service and that shock has caused Sir Jocelyn to die of heart failure — what an unlucky taint there is in that family.

From Mark Wyndham, RAC Base Depot, M.E.F. 11 April 1943.

. . . I do think it funny Bruce acting — he has never stopped since he was born . . . My new Boss I am told has a daughter called by most 'The Sherman' (kind of tank) who is a very physical young lady so God knows what I am in for. I shall probably be sacked within a fortnight like many others who have held similar appointments.

To my mother from John Wyndham, with Harold Macmillan in Algiers. Undated.

Dearest Mamma, Lady Dorothy has arrived. I like her so much. But whether she will like being here I don't know. There is a slight aimlessness about the visit. Algeria, however, is looking so pretty at this time of the year, with her blue sky and sea and all the blossoms and the flowers and the vines in leaf and the mountains behind, that maybe Lady Dorothy will be attracted by it.

She arrived the day before yesterday, in the afternoon, having spent the previous night in the airplane on water. She was greeted at the airfield by me, and at the villa by uncle Harold and the immediate prospect of a dinner party for an Australian

---

[1] My mother

newspaper owner passing through called Sir Keith Murdoch. It was, naturally, rather dull. Hermione Ranfurly, who was one of the guests, asked eccentrically if she might bring her pet parrot. I said no. But I cannot aver that bird, if it had come, would have debased very much the standard of conversation.

And so the regime of the new chatelaine of the Villa Desjoyaux was launched.

Mr Harold Nicolson is visiting these parts, lecturing, at the request of the Ministry of Information. He is being a great success. He has two lectures: 'The Last Peace and the Next' and 'Proust'. He dishes out whichever he thinks will suit the audience of the moment.

He addresses his letters home to his wife to 'The Hon. Vita Sackville-West' as if he was living in sin with her.

Nita. You ask if she was honest with me. The tears she shed when we parted were not feigned. She's a marvellous cook, but has no idea of how to make the rations last (used the week's butter ration to make a sauce for Monday night's dinner). And it is a mistake to employ her if there are going to be other servants in the household. She went after Andrew [Cavendish]'s servant with a kitchen knife.

I wonder who the man with the trying mother and the agreeable views can be whose biography you are sending me? I give it up, but shall look forward to the book. Thank you so much.

I gather that while Aunt Violet [Leconfield] is all right now, we can reckon on her being off her head again by next September. I believe that, according to her husband, it goes in cycles that way . . .

Best love from John.

From Mark Wyndham, RAC Base Depot. 18 July 1943.

I have been graded fit once more and am back at the above address from Alex. I have now got to do a two months' signal course here which is infuriating as I hoped to return and see my chums, although they are not busy at the moment. Had a drink with Frances last night in Shepherds. she was going out with a Gent in the Rifle Brigade with a strange name. Frances said that Ann had written to say that Egghead was concerned because

Frances was engaged to Gerry Wellesley!! The reason being that
Frances had met him while on leave and sent a joint PC to
Mummy. So if you want to cause a bit of fun just get some
strange young man to write a few words on a post card and then
you write something and send it to our mum. Then in the eyes of
our uncle you are engaged. I am going to find some black woman
to write one on, just to make 'em sit up a bit.

Our cousin, Henry Yorke, who wrote novels under the
pseudonym of Henry Green, published in 1943 one, *Caught*, on
the theme of a man who had sexual intercourse in the dark with his
sister, under the misapprehension that she was an entirely different
woman. The sister was so astounded at what was happening to her
that she was unable to find breath to enlighten him regarding his
mistake, of which he remained entirely unaware. The subject
provoked a good deal of discussion. Female disputants were, not
unnaturally, of the opinion that it was bad news if, to a man
satisfying his sexual appetite, all cats were indeed grey in the night
without a single distinguishing individual feature.

From Mark Wyndham, RAC Base Depot M.E.F.
10 August 1943.

Mummy has just sent me a letter of yours discussing Henry
Yorke's new novel and the main theme therein. I must admit it
is original, but like you I am doubtful as to the possibility of the
thing because, when you come to think of it, *no* night is so dark
one could not recognise someone at a range of zero, unless of
course he kept his eyes shut throughout the whole business. I
should love to discuss it with you and Daddy and John and Aunt
Midge. Smelling salts would be necessary in a very short time.
The whole business reminds me of the story of Lot's daughters
who got him very tight and then one of them jumped into bed
with him. The next day she told her younger sister that it was
'guise' which in Arabic means a bit of all right. So the younger
sister did the same thing the next night and cunning old Lot
pretended he was so whistled that he did not know it had
happened until his daughters started the tribes of Amorites and,
I think, Hittites.

I received a spate of letters from Egghead, type-written in capital letters from Bombay, where he was stationed, complaining that it was not like Yarmouth, from where he had been reposted. He was also in a state of deep anxiety about every notion he could possibly conjure up: the war, the future, his relatives, the unsympathetic character of the people around him — to whom my heart went out! They make very tedious reading and were impossible to answer. Frances distancing herslf from her family was a particular sorrow to him, as he was devoted to her; chiefly, I think, because she was the favourite niece of his favourite cousin 'Pry' Miller Mundy.

From Joan Hirsch at Barnard Castle. September 24 1943.

Ann [Meyrick, her sister] and her little brood left about ten days ago. I miss her very much. She arrived back at Hinton on the 15th and George walked into the drawing room on the 16th having landed at Poole by air from Egypt. So it was lucky she just got home in time. The fascinating Rupert Byass left here without paying his mess bill, a not very large sum, however there was a good deal of 'I told you so' going on about it. But I am glad to be able to say his honour was saved by Mrs Most-Dangerous-Woman-in-London Byass who rang up the mess personally to say he had asked her to send a cheque for him as in the hurry of departure he had completely forgotten to do so himself.

I read *Still as a Stranger* and found it attractive. Try *A Well Full of Leaves* by Elizabeth Myers. Rather purple patches but strong meat and full of incident. I am ashamed to say I haven't got a Bible. Everyone reads it sooner or later and loves it. I do mean to. My life is so material at the moment I feel I must do something to get onto a more spiritual plane. How does one do that? I spend my time thinking of nothing but boring household and nursery affairs. I wish I could have something else to switch on to occasionally.

How right the Italian farmworkers are not to want to go back, they would indeed be involved in more fighting. It sounded so exciting and full of promise when Italy gave in but it all seems to be rather disappointing. There we are still battling

on just the same as ever. And I daresay it will take ages to get rid
of the Germans. In fact having at one time imagined that the war
would be over by the end of this year, I am now plunged in
gloom and can't see the end at all. Henry Abel Smith, who is a
friend of Mr Churchill's told Jack that Mr C had said if all our
plans are successful and every single thing goes right for us the
war in Europe may end by Christmas. I don't suppose everything
has gone right, though. Anyway I am thankful we have not got
that fat Mussolini to keep in ease and comfort awaiting trial
when the War's over. I don't envy him being in Germany at
Hitler's mercy.

From Bruce Shand, Offlag IX A/H, Germany. 12 October 1943.

Could you be very kind and forward to Mark a letter that I am
sending c/o you? I heard from him and he assures me he is
reading Lord Chesterfield most assiduously. I am trying vainly
to recall the blasphemy mentioned in your letter which has so
shocked Mrs Hirsch, tho' I feel that remarks made in such
circumstances, as it apparently was, should be spared immor-
tality! Joan, I trust, has not been too much 'bouleversée' by the
devastating Byass charm. Thank you, as ever, for writing. Can it
be that this interminable struggle appears to be entering its final
stages, or is it another hallucination?

There was a sort of hysteria among those accustomed to being
waited on hand and foot lest their invaluable attendants might
desert them, and the enslavers were rapidly becoming the enslaved.
My mother writes a rambling letter from Gloucestershire where
she was staying with an old friend, Edward Greene. They appeared
to be pooling their domestic staff. She begins by referring to
conditions in my lodgings owned by another old friend of hers,
Blanche, Lady Lloyd:

What terrible nonsense that you can't have dinner now at Clouds
Hill. What do you do? Go without? I find just the same sort of
'nonsenses' existing here, and for real ridiculous fuss I
recommend you to an elderly bachelor! But I have to *stifle* it as if I
let it — the irritation — once get hold, there would be no end.

The job cook arrives this weekend for 3 weeks, and then E. has a permanent one coming — Whiteley went off on her hols, and we are left with Alice [my mother's housemaid] and E.'s old butler, pensioned and now returned, an *excellent* servant but I understand 'difficult', but up to now charming to me, and gets on with A. But I doubt he and W. existing comfortably side by side for long. So something has to be thought out for her, at the moment all I can think of is her going back on board wages to London — she is longing to, so she says.

We went to church at Shipton Moyne — charming name — Jack Gibb's church — *packed* and the kind of service I like — good organ and choir and he preached an excellent *short* sermon and we went into the rectory after, and all the congregation gathered there; I had a long crack with Mrs Kingscote — mother of Hugh Brassey's wife — we'd come together before, as I was staying here when her nephew, 9th Lancer Robin K., was killed, and Henry liked him so, and then she wrote me about H. and so it's gone on. She'd been over to see Gerald Grosvenor in hospital, badly wounded in tail *and* tummy, but at first all said 'slightly', as his mother [Lady Mabel Stubber] is dying and she mustn't hear. It's so sad for poor tiresome little Mac Stubber [husband]: Mab dying upstairs, John Stubber [son] just gone to Normandy and he has to keep up the fiction that Mab is hardly ill at all — to her — that Gerald is slightly wounded and John S. still in this country — a nightmare. Mab may be dead in a week, not cancer but something that makes her feel permanently *very* sick.

Michael Crighton's chorus-girl-from-USA-wife just arrived in this country and all his family agog to see her and make her acquaintance.

From Margaret Wyndham, Badminton, Glos. 6 December 1943.

I fear this will find you in bed with the inevitable 'flu — I hope nothing worse. Mary Beaufort has gone down with it today after a most strenuous Sunday. She gets up every morning to milk her cows at 7.15 and yesterday morning it was discovered they had strayed and were dotted about. Master collected them on a bicycle, but of course the milking was late and she spent the day catching up with time, and as luck would have it her land girl was having the week off! The Princess Royal has just left. It is always nice to have her. She is such fun and removes some of the 'leaf mould' which settles on us here. I have written and ordered *Reader's Digest* to be sent you. What a good idea for a present . . . .

So John is in Italy. I hope he will not be drowned in the ceaseless rain the papers speak of. I see Doll Bruntisfield has been robbed of her jewels and guns. 'The Dandies', as the police say the gang is called, is having a delightful and profitable time, indeed. What fun it must be to drop in on somebody's flat and remove the valuables — but not moral, like so much that is fun!

This was Aunt Maggie's notion of being modern and daring. I once ventured to ask somebody else in royal service why Queen Mary had put up for so many years with Aunt Maggie's rather pathetic pretentiousness? I received a pitying look and the reply: "Good heavens! You don't suppose the Royal Family cares what anybody who works for them is *like*. All they want is the job done, all the time and at any time."

From Mark Wyndham, XII R. Lancers, B.N.A.F.
15 December 1943.

Humphrey Clinker has just arrived. I have often read Smollet in anthologies but never met him in the whole so I am delighted to have a chance. John came to Din on Sunday. I dined with him last night at the villa, his boss being away. I have to go before a selection board on Monday to see if I am fit to be a regular officer. I believe you are literally made to put square pegs in round holes.

This district is madly gay. Parties every night. I am off to one tonight in the Big City. Last week Jack Price and his Boys gave a party and I did not get back till ten the next morning. The damn car broke down and we had to be towed in — not a very funny experience. We give a party next Wednesday on which I have been working for the last week, trying to turn a hall that looks like St Pancras Public Lavatory into a respectable warm place.

My breast now supports two decorations as in the last week I was honoured by the North African Star being issued with the bread and cigarette ration for the week. It clashes a bit, being a bright yellow, like the sand of the desert I am told.

From Mark Wyndham, XII R. Lancers, B.N.A.F. 22 January 1944.

I hoped Egghead would pass this way, but if he did it was at dead
of night with muffled boots and he could not have blown his nose
because Algiers is still standing. The *Tatler* and *Country Life*
arrived today from I know not who. One contained a picture of
Aunt Violet and the other a picture of David Laurie looking very
fat and bloated. 'Blighty' can't do anybody any good who has
been out East for a time. I thought Aunt Violet looked much the
same as she always did. I expected to see a weak minded,
goggle-eyed lunatic from all Mummy reports. Have you a nice
photograph of someone interesting like Mummy or yourself to
send to me? Mummy sent me a photograph of Henry which I put
in a frame, but have no picture to put in the opposite side of the
frame which is a double one. At the moment there is a picture of
Alexandria lighthouse which was sold with the frame.

From Mark Wyndham, XII R. Lancers, C.M.F. 13 June 1944.

Your useful tips have not arrived in time. Rome is a very fine city
and in particular St Peter's. The architecture is good but the
inside is a little spoilt by the ornateness of Roman Catholicism.
The Colosseum is disappointing and not as good as the one in
Nimes in France and El Dgemm (?) in Tunisia. The one at El
Dgem (?) is particularly fine as it rises alone out of an undulating
plain of olive trees and corn. Rome itself is clean and has gay
shops with girls in the streets all prettily dressed in summer
frocks which are refreshing to see. The city has escaped damage
except for the railway yards on the outskirts which give credit to
our precision bombing. I should say that in peace time Rome is
far finer than Naples, although one escaped all destruction while
the other is not its former self.

From Mark Wyndham, XII R. Lancers, C.M.F. 4 July 1944.

So enjoyed your letter about Florence which you humbly called a
deadly epistle. Tat Brinton and I had only been talking about
the delights of the OT so when I showed him your passage he
was thrilled and confessed he did not know it although a great

fan of Ecclesiasticus[1] and all the Apochrypha. Alas, by some
mishap I left my Bible with my base kit.

Micky de Pino was killed yesterday, which is very
depressing. He was my best friend and you would have liked
him and enjoyed his wit. We always thought of the time we
would have back in England together under sane conditions, but
if one had to live in insane conditions Micky was the person I
should have chosen to do it with.

I hope you do not mind, I gave your letter to Tat Brinton to
read. This is not a habit of mine, but the Bible cutting was what
I particularly wanted him to see. He was most struck by the wit
and intelligence of the whole letter and said pompously so few
girls these days would have heard of Lorenzo the Magnificent[2] (I
hadn't). Tat is about your age and pretty intelligent himself. He
agreed with me about the Colosseum, so you must take a trip to
Tunis after the war and board the light railway to Sousse. There
you will change trains and carry on your journey towards Sfax
and there, about thirty miles from that city, you will see El
Dgem Arena rising out of a flat plain and looking far more
magnificent than that at Rome, and in better repair. I await
eagerly Florence where I will look up Lorenzo the Magnificent
after your letter of introduction.
PS El Dgem trip reminiscent of Cobbet?!

*Mark Wyndham to his mother, XII R. Lancers CMF.
1 September 1944.*

John Stimpson gave Billy Willson, Michael Bradstock and
myself a lift here from Rome in his boss's private plane. He sent
our jeep on ahead to meet us at the airfield, but alas the Pope
caused trouble again as the jeep got three punctures and we
arrived at the airfield and no jeep to be seen so we had to

[1] Possibly "There are three sorts of men my soul hateth and I am much
offendeth at their way of life. A rich man that is proud, a poor man that is a liar
and an old adulterer that doteth."
[2] I just happened to fall lastingly in love with Lorenzo on my first visit to
Florence, although I don't care for ugly men. I never go into the Duomo without
thinking of where his brother was murdered and Lorenzo escaped by the skin of
his teeth.

hitch-hike on, rather a downfall having started in *our* private plane.

Rome was very hot and there was no hot water and the plug did not always pull but apart from that everything was fine. Food was delicious but terribly expensive: £2 for dinner, but well worth it for three days. One could feed cheaper and adequately, but as were on leave we patronised the posh places. Another friend I met was Claud Scott. He was with Neil Speke. He lookes just the same and is second-in-command of his Regiment. I do hope that soon our advance in France will put a stop to the Doodle-Bugs and then you will be able to return to your Flat. I hope you enjoyed your time at Clovelly. I am sending some photographs to Ursula. I hope she will send them to you. They are only happy snaps, but quite amusing.

From Mark Wyndham, XII R. Lancers, CMF. 6 November 1944.

I have not written for ages. We are up to our socks in mud here, but are now situated on a stud farm — two bulls and a bore (*sic*). Whenever a cow or sow come down the road the alarm goes up and people rush out from their cars to enjoy the exhibition. I saw a sow go by yesterday and raised the alarm. The door of the Intelligence officers' truck was flung open and out came Alan Carson saying 'Where, Where?'. Men went running out of the cook house. It all helps to break the monotony. I hear elephants have to breed in swamps to minimise the height of the lady elephant.

Heard from John yesterday, now back at work after jaundice. He tried to come up here on his sick leave but could not get transport. Perhaps it was a good thing as for the last month we have been very uncomfortable and not in the usual Palace that we manage to get into. Please note the new army commander is a XII lancer. John Stimpson has gone to Burma with Oliver Leese.

From Mark Wyndham, XII R. Lancers, CMF.
29 November 1944.

. . . I still can't see myself settling down to farming. You are absolutely correct that I have a low opinion of my capabilities, possibly no lower than they actually are, but as you say, if I had a *higher* opinion than they actually are, like Monty, it might bring them up to, or nearly up to, that opinion . . .

Mummy writes that Guest Keen and Nettlefold are iron masters which would entail hard work in an office in Cardiff or the like. This does not appal me as much as it might, even though I do not know what iron masters are, unless it is something like Dorman Long. I shall bear it in mind and try to get more data about it. I have plenty of time as my demobilising group is fairly high (33) on Account of my age, so I shall have to soldier on for a bit. I hear John is off to America, luckly little fellah. We have left the stud farm so things are pretty dull now."

From Mark Wyndham, XII R. Lancers, CMF. 2 December 1944.

I have been to Florence but forgot all you said and did not meet any of the things you advised. The stay was supposed to be only 24 hours, but as all the powers that be were out to Dinner the night before, we set off that night and had a long moonlight drive, arriving in the city at half past eleven. We stayed at the Palazzo of our Italian liaison officer Rudolpho Geddes. It was strange walking into this house with a dining room that might have been in London. Glass chandeliers, eighteenth century French furniture, and flowers and knick-knacks, snuff boxes, etc, on the tables. Rudolpho's wife was there and his Mother, a typical old chic Italian lady with red hair who wore a lot of dead weight on her wrists and fingers and large fantastic hats on her head and never stopped talking Italian and bad French. The servant wore a white coat with buttons covered in coronets. He was always drunk and once when the Contessa — the mother — came into the room he said, 'Oh, what a beautiful lady'. She replied "You know who I am, you must be drunk', and chucked her umbrella at him!!

That night several girls came in and we danced to a gramophone. The girls were all quite attractive and very well dressed and spoke English very well. It seemed all very strange to see these girls of a defeated nation looking neat and tidy and gay when one knew one's own country was pretty shabby and all the girls were working like mad. I found it difficult to make conversation to these girls and really was a little bored in their company. I was *not* a social success. The house was not nice and although I was impressed by the drawing room at first sight, it had no curtains or pelmets or any sign of them ever being there.

I did extensive shopping in the town and spent a fortune on gifts for you and Mamma. I did not go into the cathedral and all the picture galleries were closed. I saw the Ponte Vecchio in the distance — all the other bridges were Baileys. Several of the Italians I met knew Mrs Parrish[1]. That is the extent of my impressions.

Rudolpho was most hospitable but I find I cannot get on well with Italians. I am of the old school that believe black men start at Calais and foreigners at Dover . . . . Got a letter from Nan today saying lady Dorothy had had a baby, is this Dot Head? I thought she had had all the children she wanted long ago. I have sent by ordinary post a cutting out of eighth army news on the Regiment, telling of all our exploits in the last six months. It is quite a 'Bum up' but it is true with no exaggerations. Hope you like the bag and scarves when they arrive.

From Mark Wyndham, CMF. 23 January 1945.

Last weekend I long-hopped to Rome and stayed one night with John in fantastic luxury. Uncle Harold was away so we were the only two in the house. We had Dan and Hermione Ranfurly to Dinner. I was called at nine next morning with Breakfast, Egg and all, and was told that when I had finished that my bath would be 'drawn'. Scotch whisky was in abundance and very good food — what a rest cure — I hope to go back for some more at the end of my course. John is very house proud. It is hideous inside on account of belonging to the Fascist Minister of Works. John made me on arrival do some extensive furniture removing with some 'pieces' he had stolen off the Embassy. Tony Nutting and a very nice man called John Mallet came to lunch and afterwards we visited the Colosseum of which you know my views. Then I had to hurry away to catch my lorry.

The following letter from my mother, written in her best inconsequential style, which was very popular with her host of

---

[1] Mrs Huntingdon's mother. A notable American hostess in Florence.

correspondents ("You write just like you talk, Gladdie, it's like having a conversation with you!") describes her return to London from Gloucestershire.

From my mother. 13 September, 1944.

I got here on Monday. *Such* a journey, the Train arrived at Chippenham packed with the whole of the children of London — or so it look'd — Alice managed, by squeezing, to get standing room in a carriage of 16! I gave it up and settled to wait for the next, when a place in a 1st class was made for me — 10 of us — and I found I was in with Sir H. and Ly Knatchbull Hugessen, just flown back from Ankara — one night in Cairo and the next at Gib. — and you should have seen how eagerly they peered out of the windows — drinking in the landscape — She dressed in cotton and mufflers and overcoats and rugs over it all, and said the heat in Cairo was stifling — He to go on to Brussels *at once* — I longed to ask re. the horrid wily Turks, but of course I didn't. A woman practically sitting on my lap said she'd landed by air from Nyassaland that morning after 6 years out of England — I'd somehow got into the carriage reserved for aeroplane passengers from Bristol.

I flew to the Registry Offices and Have Been given the names of 2 Cooks who unfortunately can't be 'seen' till next week (if they are willing *then*). . . . I talked to Ruth [her sister-in-law] on the telephone . . . . She says Humphrey's Home Guard will have ended — he expects — by Nov — and then they'll give up the flat and she'll come up daily to the Red X — who, if General Horrocks is to be believed?, will Be Wanted more than Ever? — with this fighting 'every inch of the way to Berlin' — she said Mary's boy friend had written really charming letters and seen David's grave and put flowers on it and given them many details, etc . . . .

I go to tea today with Maud to see the flat, and they now sleep in their beds, and enjoy it to the full — instead of on a row of mattresses in the passage. However, the Rocket Gun is supposed to be in full Swing, only you mayn't mention it (on the pain of Death) to keep the Germans Guessing, one Missile fell in Chiswick and caused a Small Earth Quake, But only Killed 7 people, and fell 40ft into the Ground; the Authorities Give out that it was the Gas meter Blowing up! But I can't see what they'll say when the next one falls? 'They' start in the Hartz Mts, and go 40 miles into the air, — and Generally Blow up there, But should They manage to Reach Here, they do, as you can imagine, a Good Deal of Damage, But it's said the Germans Haven't yet managed to 'Perfect' one — all very disagreeable and possibly untrue — But this is What is Being Bandied Round London at the moment. I certainly was woken by a Great Bang on Tuesday about 6 and then later another one occurred, But it may Have Been Something far Less terrific than this Missile? and I Haven't Been to Chiswick to investigate, So Don't Vouch for its Truth. But I Do feel it's so foolish of the parents of Children to Bring them Back at the moment.

From Margaret Wyndham, Badminton, Glos. 23 October 1944.

I would have written sooner, but have been kept rather close in Waiting, besides being rather tired after two long motor drives in one day — the late one in the blackout watching the little red light of the Police Car in front.

The Christening [of Prince Richard, now Duke of Gloucester] was a very pleasant meeting. Delia Peel was in Waiting and asked *most* affectionately after you who she greatly admires! The Royal Family and the Scotts had lunch together; the Scott family including the Duke and Duchess of Buccleuch, their son and a very pretty Wren daughter Elizabeth and the Duchess of Gloucester's two sisters, Mida Hawkins and Sybil Phipps and her daughter Eileen Phipps who is going to Australia with her Aunt. I joined the Household luncheon and then we adjourned to the Private Chapel. The Gloucesters' Household and the Staff they are taking to Australia came down by train in time for the Christening.

The baby wore the family Christening robe made originally for Queen Victoria's eldest child, and was christened in the small gold font made equally for the Empress Frederick's baptism. Prince Richard had good lungs and made use of them as soon as Lord Lang had him in his arms. The Archbishop of Canterbury, with 'an infection in his legs', another name for gout, was too ill to officiate. We then adjourned to the two big drawing rooms, where we all mingled, but I had the opportunity of telling the Duke of Gloucester of the fine plane your firm were building for him. Princess Elizabeth looked and was charming. Sandy Ramsay has grown very tall and managed his new leg very well. How his mother does worship him! He is going to Australia as you know with the Gloucesters.

We were fed on coffee and Christening cake. It sounds inadequate, but I found I did not want tea later as it came so soon after lunch. It rained all the time we drove to Windsor and part of the time coming back. In fact we have little but rain here. Princess Arthur of Connaught brought a decorative but rather vulgar sicknurse with her. We all wondered who she was and eventually the Air Equerry brought her to Delia's room where we noticed she had no stockings on, but had painted her legs to give the impression they were there.

The King of Greece arrived late for lunch, having lost his way between London and Windsor. I could not imagine how he had done this on the Bath Road, but I heard he had made a detour to avoid an American convoy and got lost in lanes.

EPILOGUE

ABOUT TWENTY YEARS AGO motoring through Stamford, I turned aside, on impulse, and took, for the first time in forty years, the road to Laxton — that absurdly grand, but enchanting home of my early youth, to which I had never ceased to bear allegiance, in preference to any other house that I had subsequently looked upon as home. I drove my car past the grand entrance lodge, which had been closed and locked and the drive overgrown with grass even in my day, and turning in at the farm entrance, proceeded up the long drive through the park, noting the ice-house, set in the bank beside the road, half-way between the highroad and the house. The immediate surroundings of the house seemed even more neglected than in my parents' time. Getting out of the car at the front door, I recognised, as though seeing a forgotten friend, the giant beech tree still standing, a hundred yards beyond the house.

An old monk in a brown habit opened the door. I explained my presence; he welcomed me warmly and said the house was now a training school for the Roman Catholic priesthood. We stepped into the stone hall. I, with my adult eyes, was overwhelmed by its size and stateliness.

171

My escort saw his surroundings with the accepting, unquestioning eyes of the child that I had once been.

Of the nine reception rooms on the ground floor, my parents had appropriated four to form a suite of bedroom, dressing room, bathroom and sitting room. The windows to the bedroom looked out on an enclosed court which was known as the Cockatoo Garden. That bedroom was now a none-too-clean and disorderly kitchen. A jumble of kitchen and other equipment blocked the view to the Cockatoo Garden.

I particularly asked to be shown the bedroom on the mezzanine floor, with the jungle wallpaper — the scene of my childish terrors. As I feared, the jungle motif had gone. The walls were now painted a grubby beige. The dining room, to the left of the entrance hall, with three tall windows overlooking the park, was the only room that remained at all as I remembered it. There I was surprised by a chimneypiece of ugly dark grey marble. I could not recollect the design of the chimneypiece from my parents' day, any more than I could remember the minutiae of my father's appearance without his clothes, but I would have expected my mother, with her conscious good taste, to have installed a more pleasing fitment.

The old monk was anxious to know the history of the house. All I could tell him was that it had been built in 1798, but by whom and for whom I did not know. The original purpose had been very different from the one it was now serving. A better purpose than a stately home.

And yet . . . in the present dinginess that the dignified stone walls contained, it had lost that sense of being the background for continuing generations of a family whose roots, however far the individual travelled, remained in thought and loyalty gripped in some small acreage of English land.

INDEX

Aarons, Dr 16
Abel-Smith, Anthony 129
Abel-Smith, Henry 160
Acheson, Mary 40
Acheson, Patrick 40
Alexander, Brenda 76, 92–3, 105–12, 115–17, 131; letters 145, 146
Alexander, Col 76, 117
Alexander, Mrs 76, 116
Allen, Woody 91
Anglesey, Marquess of 68–9
Anglesey, Marchioness of 68–9, 71
Ashley, Edwina 123
Asquith, Raymond 82, 83

Baird, Charlotte (afterwards Countess of Enniskillen) 50, 51, 57
Balfour, A. J. 33, 34, 35, 36, 38, 39
Beaufort, Duke & Duchess of 177
Beresford, Lord Charles 83
Bingham, Rose 26
Birley, Maxine 161
Blunt, Mary 52
Blunt, Wilfrid Scawen 32, 39
Bonsor brothers, the 17
Bowles, Andy 50
Bradstocke, Michael 164
Brinton, Tat 163, 164
Brodrick, Guinevere 27
Brodrick, Mary Emma 49, 50
Browning, Oscar 120
Bruce, Beryl 129, 152
Bruntisfield, Dorothy, Lady 162
Buccleuch, Duke & Duchess of 169
Byass, Rupert 159

Byass, Mrs R. 159, 160
Byron, Lord 120
Byron, Lady 120–21

Carson, Alan 165
Casamajor, Jane 49
Cavendish, Andrew 157
Cavendish-Bentinck, Anne 93
Cavendish-Bentinck, Peggy 93
Chamberlain, Joseph 34
Cheetham, Lady 44
Churchill, Winston 43, 160
Churchill, Mrs Winston 43
Clifton-Brown, Mrs 141
Coates, Betty 77
Cole, Ann 41, 51, 105; letters 62–3, 140
Cole, Francis 39, 51, 53–4, 99 passim
Cole, Henry Arthur 49
Cole, John (1680–1726) 48
Cole, Kitty 51, 54, 87
Cole, Sir Lowry 49
Cole, Michael 51, 64
Cole, Sir William 48
Colquhoun, Ivor 149
Colquhoun, Lady 149
Connaught, Princess Arthur of 170
Cook, Mrs 15
Cooper, Lady Diana 26, 91, 121
Coward, Noel 122
Cradock-Hartopp, Sir John (1829–1888) 18–19
Crewe, Marchioness of 39
Crewe-Milnes, Mary 77–8

173

Curzon, Viscountess 37, 38

Daly, Diana 94–5
Danabassis, Thomas 106–07, 109
de Pino, Michael 26, 164
Devonshire, 8th Duke of 67–8
Devonshire, Evelyn, Dowager Duchess of 94–5
Donegal, Marquess of 26
Douglas-Pennant, Winifred 41, 43
Duff, Sir Michael 70

Egghead, see Farquhar, Ronald
Egremont, 3rd Earl of (1750–1837) 31
Eisenhower, General 117
Elcho, Lord, afterwards Earl of Wemyss 36, 39
Elcho, Lady 33, 35, 36, 37, 38, 39
Eliot, Elizabeth 21
Elizabeth, Princess 170
Enniskillen, 2nd Earl of 49
Enniskillen, 3rd Earl of 49
Enniskillen, 4th Earl of (1843–1923) 49, 50, 51
Enniskillen, 5th Earl of (1876–1963) 51, 52, 53, 55, 57, 58, 59, 61, 62, 84, 154, 155
Enniskillen, Irene, Countess of (m. 1907) 39, 51, 52, 53

Farquhar, Ronald 63, 100, 150, 151, 155, 157, 159
Fauchet, Mlle 86
Faunce, Miss 77
Fields, W. C. 35
Foot sisters, the 25
Ford, Billy 56

Galway, Lucia, Viscountess 91
Geddes, Rudolpho 166, 167
Gibbs, Jack 161
Gloucester, Prince Henry, Duke of 170
Gloucester, Prince Richard, Duke of 169
Gore-Booth, Brian 135–36
Gore-Booth, Hugh 156
Gore-Booth, Sir Jocelyn 63
Gosford, Mildred, Countess of 40

Graham, Dorothy 40
Graham, Harry 40
Graham, Rutherford 35
Grant-Williams, Elizabeth 129
Green, Henry 62, 72, 158
Green Mr 25
Greene, Edward 144, 160
Greene, Sir Raymond (1869–1947) 17–18, 25, 144
Grosvenor, Gerald 161

Hare, Augustus 42
Harris, Lady Frances 49
Hawkins, Lady 'Mida' 169
Head, Lady Dorothy 167
Hirsch, Joan 159, 160
Hobhouse, John Cam 120
Hornby, Rosamund 77
Horrocks, General 168
Houses named in text:
    Badminton, Glos. 161, 169
    Chartwell, Kent 43
    Croxteth Hall, Liverpool 122
    Edmondthorpe Hall, Leics. 40, 75
    Florence Court, County Fermanagh 48–52, 55–61, 62, 64, 105, 150
    Hampton Court 60
    Hardwick Hall, Derbyshire 94–5
    Laxton House, Northants. 13, 24, 58, 75, 171–72
    Petworth House, Sussex 13, 31, 32, 58
    Plas Newydd, Anglesey, 70
    Port Eliot, Cornwall 21
    Serlby Hall, Yorks. 16
    Stanway, Glos. 37, 38, 57–8
    Welbeck Woodhouse, Notts. 92–3
Huntington, Alfreda 40
Huntington, Constant 40
Huntington, Gladys 40

James, J. H. 32, 149, 154

Keppel, Mrs George 82
Kingscote, Mrs 161
Kippings, Captain 101
Knatchbull-Hugesson, Sir H. 168
Knatchbull-Hugesson, Lady 168
Knebworth, Viscount 70

Lawrence, Gertrude 122
Leconfield, 1st. Lord 32
Leconfield, 2nd Lord 32, 33, 71
Leconfield, 3rd Lord 70, 86
Leconfield, Constance, Lady 32–3, 62, 71, 77, 99–100, 102
Leconfield, Violet, Lady 70, 146, 157, 163
Leese, General Sir Oliver 165
Leslie, Sir Shane 64
Lloyd, Blanche, Lady 160
Lyttelton, Alfred 36
Lyttelton, Laura 36
Lyttelton, May 35, 36

Macguire clan 48, 64
Mackintosh, Arbell 94, 95
MacMillan, Harold 156, 183
MacMillan, Lady Dorothy 156
Mallet, John 167
Manchester, Duchess of 68, 71
Mann, Ned 151
Mary, Queen 162
Maugham, Syrie 70
Maxwell, Sir Aymer 27
Melbourne, Viscountess 120–21
Mesa, Captain 26
Mitford, Deborah 136
Mitford, Unity 136
Moisley 61
Molyneux, Major 123
Montague-Douglas-Scott, Elizabeth 169
Montgomery, General 142
Mountbatten, Lord Louis 123, 146
Muir, Judy 80
Murdoch, Miss 76

Nares, Geoffrey 26
Netherlands, Beatrix, Queen of The 60
Nicolson, Harold 157
Nita 157
Nutting, Anthony 167

Ormsby-Gore, Mary 77

Paget, Caroline 70
Parkinson, Michael 122
Peel, Lady Delia 169

Peel, Mary 80
Penn, Eric 27
Phillpotts, Ambrosine 55, 56
Phipps, Eileen 169
Phipps, Lady Sybil 169
Pigott, Miss 120
Price, Major Jack 162
Price, Jim 57
Price, John 57
Price, Sally 57

Queensberry, Marquess of 120

Ramsay, Capt. Alexander 170
Ranfurley, Earl of 167
Ranfurley, Countess of 157, 167
Revens, Mrs 142
Rickard, 21, 22
Roberts, Irene 40
Rochester, Earl of 69
Rochester, Countess of 69
Romilly, Mrs 43
Rosebery, Earl of 71
Royal, the Princess 41, 161

Salisbury, 2nd Marquess of 33
Salisbury, 3rd Marquess of 36
Scott, Claud 165
Scott, Peter 118
Sefton, Earl of 122, 123–24
Sefton, Countess of 123–24
Seymour, Horatia 41, 43, 44
Shand, Bruce 90, 135; letters 136, 137, 138, 140–41, 147–48, 150–51, 153
Shaw, Bobby 122–23
Sidgwick, Henry 34
Simpson, Mrs 88, 90, 91, 104, 123
Slater, Bob 130
Smith-Barrys, the 51
Smyly, Mrs 151
Souls, the 83
Speke, Neil 165
Stimpson, John 164, 165
Strutt, John 34
Stubber, John 161
Stubber, Major Hamilton 161
Stubber, Lady Mabel 161
Summerson, John 44
Syers, Mary 62, 150

Taylor, Alf *132, 133*
Templemore, Lord *63*
Tennant, Clare *121*
Tennant, Stephen *121–22*

Villiers, Angela *57, 63, 68*
Villiers, Helen *63, 79*
Villiers, Lady Kathleen *51, 63, 150, 156*

Waifs & Strays Society *119*
Wales, Prince of (afterwards Edward VII) *83*
Wales, Prince of (afterwards Edward VIII) *88, 90, 91, 104*
Waterfield, Gordon *103*
Webb, Beatrice *34, 35, 38*
Wellington, 7th Duke of (1885–1972) *43, 158*
White Slave Trade, the *99*
Wilde, Oscar *120*
Willes, Peter *26*
William III, King *49, 59, 60*
Willson, Billy *164*
Wrey, Florence (m. 1707) *45*
Wyndham, Edward (afterwards 5th Lord Leconfield, 1883–1967) *15, 16, 17, 18;* dinner table monologues: *19–20, 21, 24, 25, 27, 116; 117, 118, 119, 158*

Wyndham, Gladys (wife of Edward, 1885–1971) *5, 16;* attitude to children: *17, 27, 28, 79, 102, 103, 104, 116; 18–25, 43, 53, 61, 62, 77, 99–100, 119, 121, 141;* letters: *145–46, 160–61, 167–68*
Wyndham, Henry *16, 17, 19–20;* attitude to parents: *25, 116, 26, 94, 136, 137;* letters: *27, 148–49*
Wyndham, Hugh (afterwards 4th Lord Leconfield) *103, 104, 112, 148*
Wyndham, Humphrey *21, 86*
Wyndham, John *16, 18, 40, 72, 117, 136;* letters: *144, 156; 158, 162, 165, 166, 167*
Wyndham, Madeline *32, 33, 35, 72*
Wyndham, Maggie *71, 72, 80, 144, 158;* letters: *161–62, 169*
Wyndham, Mark *16, 18, 26, 40, 132, 140, 142, 143;* letters: *148, 160, 155, 156, 158, 159*
Wyndham, Maud *103, 112, 168*
Wyndham, Percy *32, 33, 35, 72*
Wyndham, Ruth *168*

Yorke, Dorothy *41, 43*
Yorke, Maud *41, 72*
Yorke, Vincent *62*